Exclusively
HARROGATE

Exclusively
HARROGATE

Malcolm G Neesam

Smith Settle

First published in November 1989 by

Smith Settle Limited
Ilkley Road
Otley
LS21 3JP

Second impression November 1989
Third impression December 1989

© Malcolm G Neesam
Colour photographs © Richard Littlewood
Foreword © Jean MacQuarrie

All rights reserved. No part of this book may
be reproduced, stored in a retrieval system,
or transmitted in any form or by any means,
without the prior permission of the publishers.

ISBN Paper 1 870071 41 7
Cloth 1 870071 42 5

Designed, printed and bound by
SMITH SETTLE
Ilkley Road, Otley, West Yorkshire LS21 3JP

DEDICATION

To my dear cousins, Audrey, Renée and Shirley, without whose kindness and hospitality my researches in London could not have been done.

ACKNOWLEDGEMENTS

The author acknowledges the expertise of photographer Richard Littlewood who produced most of the colour plates, and records his thanks to all who co-operated with the provision of other photographs or information, especially –

Harrogate Borough Council
Mr M Hine
Mrs M Jehangir
Dr and Mrs C Nicholson
Brigadier and Mrs W F Ridley
Harrogate Theatre

Permission is gratefully acknowledged to quote from the following, *Edward Elgar: The Windflower Letters* (Oxford University Press 1989).

Photographic Acknowledgements

The Mansell Collection, p82 (top); National Portrait Gallery, p7 (top right), p8, p12, p13, p24, p41, p49 (left); National Railway Museum, front cover, p102-3, p116; Harrogate Resort Services Department, p68, p133 (top right).

All remaining material is copyright to the Walker-Neesam Archive

FOREWORD

Malcolm Neesam's writings and lectures on the history of Harrogate and the colourful characters who helped to shape the town have enthralled the residents of Harrogate for many years.

Now, with the publication of *Exclusively Harrogate*, Mr Neesam's extensive knowledge of our beautiful town will be shared and enjoyed by a wider audience. The author has the rare gift of being able to put the flesh on the bones of our history, to paint a lively picture of times past, and to draw some interesting parallels with present day happenings!

Exclusively Harrogate tells the story of this North Yorkshire town which developed a reputation as one of the finest spa resorts in the world.

Mr Neesam's animated style of writing brings to life those distant days of gracious living when being seen at the right places, with the right people, was of paramount importance.

Harrogate was very much 'the right place' and now, more than a century later, the town still retains that image of elegance and gentility which sets it apart from any other.

Enjoy this dip into the past and learn a little about why Harrogate, now a thriving conference and tourist town, is still so very special.

Jean MacQuarrie

INTRODUCTION

Reader, be you visitor or resident, know that this town is special. You doubt it? Then apply the test. When talking with strangers in distant parts, say you come from Harrogate, and note the reaction. 'Harrogate! – isn't that rather a, well, . . . sort of place'. Precisely. The image is strong, but hard to reduce to words, or even definitions. What, for example, makes a real Harrogate person? Certainly not birth or fortune. Many born in the town chose to leave it at the first opportunity, and many with the latter attribute would not dream of using their wealth to beautify or enrich its fabric. And what of a Harrogate accent? Bradford, Hull, Leeds and Wakefield all have easily recognisable accents or variants of Yorkshire dialect, but not Harrogate. Here is a town endowed by nature with the richest variety of natural mineral springs in the world, which once called itself 'The World's Greatest Spa' but which today crams the shelves of its shops and supermarkets with inferior foreign waters and allows its own to slumber in utter neglect. Here too is a town at the centre of a district which contains some of the most magnificent scenery and historic attractions in Great Britain, which has next to no unemployment, one of the best growth rates in the nation and which is set on the road towards boundless economic prosperity, and yet which is the focus for all the inter-community squabbling and party politicking in the district. The anomalies and contradictions are legion.

I shall try to explain something of the town that is Harrogate; to describe its history and what it has to offer; possibly I will establish a bond with you, which will make you determined to investigate further, to understand, to question; and possibly, if you are attentive, a secret will be revealed.

Explore Harrogate by foot, and follow the route of the town trail past the great stone monuments and terraces of Georgian and Victorian times, round the greensward of the Stray which interpenetrates the buildings as does the sea the coast. Ignore if possible the horrible metallic litter which bestrews each gutter and driveway, and imagine a time when the horse dominated transport, when the air was always pure (it's still wonderful away from the traffic), and when a more leisurely pace of life prevailed.

A comparison of Harrogate with other towns reveals evidence of a golden tomorrow, a prosperous, self-confident today, and a great past. This ordering of impressions is deliberate, and typifies the town's attitude to priorities. The elegant pump rooms and baths, the monumental public buildings, the splendid hotels, the choice houses, the broad tree-lined streets, all betoken a belief in tomorrow, in the imposition of order over chaos. Other communities may walk with their backs to the sun, glorying in the fading embers of long-dead greatness. Harrogate's way has always been progressive, looking to the future. Its day is always tomorrow.

The earliest evidence to survive for the existence of a community called Harrogate lies in the roll for the Knaresborough Court of 1332, in the sixth year of Edward II. The fact that this roll is the earliest to have survived may indicate that at some period between the compilation of the Domesday Book in 1086, which contains no reference to Harrogate, and the compilation of the court roll (now known as D L 30/488/11) which refers to John of Harrogate, the community came into being. The likelihood is that Harrogate existed as a place name for centuries before a population grew around it. The word is believed to derive from the Anglo-Norse *Here-gatte*, or 'the way to the hill of the soldier', where Herelaw (or Harlow) is the hill of the soldier and gatte (or gate) is the way (as in Stonegate in York – 'the way for the stone'). Whatever the etymology, Harrogate as a community was established by the early 1300's.

The locality was that of the great Royal Forest, which came to be known as the Forest of Knaresborough, probably because of the importance of the royal castle and the honour court. It is not known when the Royal Forest was created, but the first reference to it seems to be in the pipe roll for 1167. The Royal Forest was Crown property and so the earliest clearings and building undertaken in the Harrogate area were either done illicitly, or with Crown sanction obtained through the court and usually accompanied by payment of a fine. Although known as forest, the term 'waste' was also used, and both words imply a status different to the reality. For this Royal Forest was neither a thickly wooded park, nor an arid desert, the result of devastation wrought by the invading Scots who burned Pannal during their incursions in 1318. Instead, it was a mixture of open heath covered with rough vegetation such as gorse and bracken, with a few special plantations for timber and game (such as Oakdale, Bilton and Haverah Parks) and a scattering of farms and hamlets. The circumstances behind the growth of the tiny Harrogate community were not therefore particularly auspicious.

The fact that the earliest accounts of life in Harrogate are taken from the rolls of the honour court is reason for our knowledge being restricted to quarrels and disputes, activities not unknown to the observer of modern Harrogate. These disputes were usually over boundaries or produce. In 1347, for example, Adam de Roudon was accused of taking marl from Robert Brown's land in Bilton by means of a cart, and Brown claimed a shilling damages. These petty matters were eclipsed the following year when occurred the greatest catastrophe ever to strike Harrogate. The pestilence arrived.

The bubonic plague reached the south of England in summer 1348 and spread as far as York by late May 1349. By July it reached Knaresborough, and from thence raged throughout the forest, probably reaching Harrogate by early August. This was almost one year since Archbishop Zouche proclaimed the imminence of a great pestilence from Cawood Castle. It is therefore likely that the Harrogate citizenry were dreadfully aware of the frightfulness lurching towards them.

The effects of bubonic plague are horrible, and to a primitive population deep in the night of medieval superstition they must have seemed a visitation from hell. Many communities gave up altogether and abandoned homes, hard-won farms cleared in the forest and the graves of their forbearers, moving on to remoter regions as yet untouched by the frightful pestilence. Although it has been calculated that 48 per cent of the 575 acres of Bilton-with-Harrogate were held by tenants whose deaths are recorded in the court rolls, most of this land was taken over by remaining relatives who refused to quit. Other communities in the Nidderdale area saw much of the land vacated by death being inherited by non-relatives, which indicated that whole families had been destroyed or had fled. The steadfastness of the Harrogate citizens in the face of this calamity is the first evidence of a remarkable will to survive.

The theory that the name Harrogate predates the establishment of a community and was simply a geographical or field name is given support by the fact that the two villages which developed were not given separate names, but called High and Low Harrogate. Tradition has awarded the palm to High Harrogate, whereas Low Harrogate is regarded as having come into existence at some point in the sixteenth or seventeenth centuries. And this is not without justification, for it was at High Harrogate that the major highways met, where the chantry chapel was established by 1400, where the first mineral wells were investigated and where the earliest hotels and inns were opened.

The chantry chapel, Harrogate's first building of architectural importance, has not – alas – survived, although some of its stones may yet survive in the fabric of the old High Harrogate inns and hotels. The dissolution of 1549 ensured its end. For the next 200 years the citizens would have to church themselves at either Knaresborough or Pannal. Not that public morality appears to have slackened. In 1563 the honour court recorded that five Harrogate men were each fined three shillings four pence for being 'players of painted cards, to the bad example of their neighbours and against the laws'! In the same year the principal occupation of the citizens was still agriculture, a fact demonstrated by the fee farm rents paid by the district to the Crown: Birstwith paid £9.18.7¾ per annum, and Hampsthwaite paid £4.18.10½; Harrogate paid £12.9.2¼.

Eight years later, in 1571, an event occurred which

The Tewit Well, scene of Mr Slingsby's discovery in 1571.

was to transform Harrogate, and send it on its way of success. Mr William Slingsby discovered the Tewit Well.

Later generations confused plain Mr William Slingsby with his nephew, Sir William Slingsby, who was only nine years old at the time of discovery. But a title always sounds impressive to the gullible and no doubt added a certain cachet to the Harrogate spa, so the error was perpetuated, even to the lovely stained glass window in the Royal Pump Room.

Mr Slingsby lived at Bilton Park for many years and no doubt sampled the water of the Tewit Well on many occasions. Later writers recorded his opinion that they were similar to the waters of Spa, in what is now Belgium.

The word spread and the Tewit Well received a

regular stream of visitors keen to sample the water. One such was Dr Timothy Bright who in about 1592 bestowed the happy name of 'The English Spaw' on the well, a fact recorded by the first writer on Harrogate, Dr Edmund Deane, whose *Spadacrene Anglica* was published in 1626.

The name 'Tewit' was given because of the tewits or pewits which used to gather at the well to feed on the mineral encrustations which formed round the well head as the water evaporated.

The increasing popularity of the Tewit Well is not hard to trace. After Slingsby's enthusiastic comments came to be known, travellers would divert their journey by a few miles to try a sample. Perhaps some early miracle cures took place, such as those recorded by later writers. Then the doctors started to take note, with Dr Deane's celebrated treatise marking the start of a new period of scientific investigation. For the locals, however, the waters probably meant little beyond being known as unsatisfactory for the land or animals. They were soon to take a different attitude.

The discovery of a second important mineral well at High Harrogate set the seal on the future growth of this part of the Harrogate area. In 1631 Michael Stanhope discovered a chalybeate or iron spring half a mile away from the Tewit Well, the quality of which he valued highly because of its 'admixture of brimstone, iron and vitriol'. Nicknamed the 'Sweet Spaw' because of its palatable taste, the well soon eclipsed the popularity of the Tewit Well, which fell into decay. Stanhope's book *Cures Without Care* of 1632 also refers to the sulphur springs of Low Harrogate, one of which he says has 'beene long knowne by the name of the stinking well'. The prime objective of the book was, however, to publicise the chalybeate springs of High Harrogate.

At the same time as these important developments were taking place, the ugly and foolish drama of religious persecution was being played out. The

The St John's Well, or Sweet Spa, seen from the site of Dr Neale's seventeenth century baths.

Catholic Sir Francis Trappes Byrnand of Harrogate Hall had to complain to the head of the compounding commission for the North that his family were again being harrassed by informers. It was a sign of worse to come. Certain Harrogate residents had their own views on the recusant 'problem'. On the 11th November 1641, Thomas Stockdale of Bilton Park wrote to Lord Fairfax about recusancy, saying 'I have heard some propound to have them all put to the sword, which, methinks, is a council better becoming a Turk than a Christian'. Bravo, Mr Stockdale. Sadly he was listed as a traitor by the Royalists and prevented from returning to Bilton Park until the capture of Knaresborough Castle in the Civil War, which broke out on the 23rd October 1642.

Harrogate historians such as Haythornthwaite have tried to show that whereas Knaresborough and York were Royalist and on the losing side, Harrogate was Parliamentarian and on the winning side. This is probably a simplification. All accounts of Harrogate's political sympathies postdate July 1644, when on Marston Moor, located between Harrogate and York, the Royalists were crushingly defeated. The peculiarly strong will to survive, which had served the Harrogate community so well 300 years earlier during the Black Death, may have played no small role in persuading the townspeople of their Parliamentary sympathies.

If the Civil War had little direct effect upon Harrogate, the same could not be said of the period following the battle of Naesby on the 14th June 1645 when Charles I was totally defeated. A petition to Parliament dated the 26th February 1646 from the inhabitants of Harrogate and all the other townships and villages within the Wapentake of Claro begged for the fortifications and garrison of Knaresborough Castle to be maintained to protect the inhabitants from 'outrages at the hands of straggling soldiers'.

On the 8th February 1646 a curious procession passed across the narrow bridge at Oak Beck, which still presents a rural visage to this part of Harrogate. King Charles I, a prisoner of the Scots, was being moved from Ripon to Wakefield on his way to being delivered over to the Parliamentarians. A local tradition, recorded by Hargrove in 1809, claimed that having past Harlow Hill and reached Burn Bridge, the king's high crowned hat was swept from his head by the branches of a great tree, the owner of which (being a Royalist) caused it to be felled in retribution.

After the re-establishment of the monarchy under Charles II in 1660, the Harrogate spa enjoyed a period of expansion. The very first public bathing house was built in about 1663 at High Harrogate next to the Sweet Spa under the supervision of Dr George Neale. The provision of warm water baths was an innovation which proved its worth and spread rapidly, being in all probability copied by the local farmers-turned-innkeepers. Indeed, according to Dr Neale's *Spadacrene Eboracensis* of circa 1693, twenty bathing houses had been established before the end of the century.

1663 saw other events take place at Harrogate, including a plot to overthrow the Government. This amateurish escapade was largely planned by Dr Edward Richardson, who had been a preacher in Ripon under the Commonwealth but who subsequently had established a medical practice in Harrogate. No more than a gathering of ill-prepared malcontents, carried away by their own enthusiasm, the plot had a short life and the authorities had little difficulty in suppressing it. Richardson escaped to Holland, but many others were arrested and imprisoned in gloomy York Castle. One such was John Sergeant of Harrogate, who was hanged.

Harrogate was a much smaller community than Knaresborough at this time, and the 1664 hearth tax returns showed that whereas Knaresborough had 156 houses Harrogate had only 57. A comparison of the number of houses with more than six hearths reveals a very interesting fact – Knaresborough had one such dwelling but Harrogate had four, and of these, two were certainly used to accommodate visitors. Standards of accommodation, however, still left much to be desired. A few years after the discovery of the Sweet Spa, the Countess of Buckingham visited Harrogate in an attempt to gain relief from asthma. Finding the local accommodation indifferent, she had a tent pitched near the Sweet Spaw, where she spent some hours every day drinking the chalybeate water at proper intervals. It is recorded that she obtained a complete cure.

A visitor less fortunate than the Countess of Buckingham was Lady Elmes, who visited Harrogate on the 4th June 1665:

'The first inst we arrived att the nasty Spaw, and have now began to drinke the horid sulfer watter, which all thowgh as bad as is posable to be immajaned, yet in my judgment plesant, to all the doings we have within doorse, the house and all that is in it being horidly nasty and crowded up with all sorte of company, which we Eate with in a roome as the spiders are redy to drope into my mouthe, and sure hath nethor been well cleaned nor ared this doseuen yerese, it makes me much moare sicke than the nasty water...'

The day of the sub-standard accommodation was, however, drawing to a close.

The early accommodation was provided by the farmers, a fact demonstrated by tracing the occupations and land use of the families and localities of the earliest known inns. In time, the farmers would have found that more profit could be had from letting their rooms to visitors than in full-time agriculture. Thus came into being the great hotels and inns of old Harrogate. The first major establishment to open was the Queen, which according to tradition dates from 1687, and which was located halfway between the two wells of High Harrogate, the Tewit Well and the St John's or Sweet Well.

Within a few years of the Queen being opened, a second major inn came on the High Harrogate scene – the Granby, which was originally called the Sinking Ship.

As these inns were built at two of the apexes of the High Harrogate 'triangle' it is hardly surprising to learn that the remaining apex was eventually provided with a third inn, the Dragon. The shape of High Harrogate was thus determined.

Low Harrogate remained in primitive condition until the eighteenth century. Although the sulphur waters of Low Harrogate had been used for some time, it was to the chalybeate springs of High Harrogate that visitors journeyed most often. The discerning, however, were beginning to take the waters of the 'Stinking Well', and some remarkable cures were recorded. On the 2nd October 1695 the antiquary Abraham de la Pryme noted:

'I was yesterday with Mr. Anderson of this town, a fine gentleman, and of a great estate. Talking of the Spaw Waters..., but especially the Sulphur Well, and of the great virtue it has, amongst other things he told me that he was there this year, and had a waiting boy with him, that for about a month before, had been subject by times to have something to rise up in his throat, and then to vomitt blood. He caryed this boy to the sulpher well, and, having made him drink heartily of the water, he vomitted up a skin, something like a bladder, full of clotted blood. It came up, he says, by pieces, at three or four vomits. This is very strange, and well worth taking notice of.'

Other – less unpleasant – cures are recorded from the earlier seventeenth century, which show that the Sulphur Well was known for its medicinal qualities from quite an early period.

The shape and later growth of Low Harrogate was determined by the ancient link from Harlow Hill to the Sulphur Well, and the siting of the first buildings in the vicinity of the well. The road link led by the spring known as the 'Cold Bath', which later supplied the road with its name. Before this apt description, the oldest known purely internal Harrogate thoroughfare had an even more evocative name – Robin Hood Lane. As for the buildings, the most substantial were the inns, of which the Crown, the White Hart and the Crescent were the oldest. The Crown – for over a century the only establishment in Low Harrogate that could hope to rival the great High Harrogate hotels – was probably a yeoman's house which was converted into an inn at some period around 1700. Its location directly in front of the Old Sulphur Well indicates an ancient establishment. The ramshackled Crescent, long vanished from Low Harrogate, has left its name in Crescent Gardens, and the handsome neo-classical structure of the White Hart today serves a function different to that of hostelry.

Further up towards Pannal from the Old Sulphur

Well lay the mysterious region known as Bogs Field, which had been partly investigated in about 1704 but which had to await the reign of Victoria for scientific analysis. Bogs Field, so called because of the marshy effect of the mineral springs surfacing in proximity, is a natural wonder of the world.

A scientific survey in the 1930's revealed that the mineral springs of Bogs Field, together with most of the other famous Harrogate springs, were not the result of rainfall and indeed were completely independent of the action of precipitation. The common cause of mineral springs is when rainfall percolates downwards through the earth until it reaches a natural drainage system, which may then pass through mineral deposits which impart the mineral content to the water, before it rises as a spring or well at the surface. At Harrogate the waters are not 'meteoric', but the result of a different process.

Superheated steam produced by a fractured and sinking mass of granite is forced upwards at great pressure, condensing before it reaches the surface. It has long been known that typical igneous rock such as granite, if thoroughly dried, may still be able to yield a considerable amount of water of constitution when distilled at a red heat. A cubic kilometre of granite treated in this manner may yield twenty-five to thirty million metric tons of water, which is enough to supply the Harrogate mineral springs for a very long period.

When the rising vapour reaches the fissures and cracks produced by the cooling magma it condenses and forms water, taking on the mineral properties of the fissures as it does so. Over a great period of time, the ascending water takes route to the surface, still retaining the unique mineral properties of the strata through which it has passed. Such water is known as magmatic or plutonic water, to indicate that it is the result of action deep beneath the earth and that it has never existed as rainfall.

Bogs Field, Valley Gardens, a wonder of the natural world.

The eighteenth century knew nothing of all this and produced several theories to account for the puzzling phenomenon of Bogs Field, the most popular of which was that the waters were the result of sunken timber rotting beneath a bed of earth and moss. From the point of smell, this explanation was not unreasonable!

By 1700 Harrogate was well established as a spa, thanks to the literary exertions of the doctors who produced pamphlets and treatises with great facility. Advice on matters other than which water to take for which ailment and in what quantity now started to appear, with special attention being given to diet and exercise. Dr French, writing in 1760, advised those with weak stomachs to first warm the waters, and to take exercise:

'In more particular manner, I forbid all flesh that is very salt, and fat, as bacon, pork neats, feet, tripes, ducks, geese, gizards of poultry, all salt fish, eels . . . I disapprove not of beef if it has been salted but a week, especially for those that love it.'

The increasing number of visitors to Harrogate in the early part of the eighteenth century led to a growing call for a church. Since the Reformation, the

The former Queen Hotel, established circa 1687, was the earliest of all the Harrogate inns.

Clive of India stayed at the Granby in 1763 where he would work on state papers at a table placed in the window of the long room.

The Crown, after substantial reconstruction in the 1840's and at the hands of George Dawson in the 1870's, would not be recognisable to Lord Byron, although standards of accommodation are as high as ever.

The lordly Granby, for centuries the top address in Harrogate.

citizens had been forced to journey either to Knaresborough or Pannal for divine service, a state of affairs which was clearly inconvenient for all concerned. Lack of any form of local government with power to raise money for the construction of a church meant that the project could be furthered only by means of voluntary contributions. These were soon forthcoming. Lady Elizabeth Hastings, a famous national philanthropist and regular visitor to Harrogate, opened a subscription with the generous gift of £50 in 1743. Others followed, and the Crown provided land at the centre of what later became High Harrogate Stray. When the new Chapel of St John's was opened in 1749, it could have been claimed without any exaggeration that it was thanks to the generosity of the visitors and the Crown, rather than to the inhabitants, that Harrogate once again had a place of worship.

One of the local characters who would have been familiar to the visitors during the 1730's and 1740's was Blind Jack, the Yorkshire roadmaker. Jack Metcalf, to give him his real name, was a citizen of Knaresborough who achieved the status of a national celebrity thanks to his efficiency as a maker of roads and highways. He was also a fiddler of no small accomplishment if contemporary accounts are anything to go by, and was in demand at the great Harrogate hotels to provide entertainment in the long rooms. A popular biography relates that Blind Jack served as an army bandsman at the battle of Falkirk in 1745, so his versatility is not to be doubted. The same biography also tells that when Jack was playing at the Granby (then known as the Royal Oak) he caught sight of the landlord's daughter, Dorothy, who was preparing for her wedding the following day. After a brief meeting, he declared his love for her and the two agreed to elope the same evening. Jack then returned to the tap room and toasted the 'Bride & Groom' to the unsuspecting company. The story goes on to describe secret

Daniel Defoe visited Harrogate around 1717 and wrote: 'We were surprised to find a great deal of good company here drinking the Waters, and indeed, more than we found afterwards at Scarborough; though this seems to be a most desolate out-of-the-world place. . . .'

lanterns, midnight rides to remote inns and of final reconciliation between Jack and the landlord. Colourful as such tales are, they were probably commonplace, as Harrogate was rapidly becoming known as a centre for lively encounters and good living. It follows that elopements would not have been uncommon in a social setting which, although officially was a magnet for the ailing, in reality assisted parents to parade their offspring in a manner best calculated to entice suitable marriage partners.

An important step towards improving facilities was taken in the 1760's by Mrs Wilks, the enterprising owner of the Granby Hotel. A barn attached to Granby Farm was converted to a theatre, and plays for the edification of patrons were provided. On the 15th August 1769, Coleman and Garrick's *Clandestine Marriage* was played, to which a farce was appended *The Virgin Unmasked, or an old man taught wisdom*. At an average price of two shillings admittance, there would have been few – if any – of the townspeople who could have afforded a ticket. And in any case, by 1769 the townspeople had a much more serious problem on their minds – the proposed enclosure of the Royal Forest.

The 1760's had seen a widespread movement towards enclosing Royal Forest land, both for the financial returns to the Crown and the freeing of large tracts of land for development by private owners. The move to enclose the Royal Forest of Knaresborough, of which Harrogate formed a part, posed a serious threat to Harrogate. All the wells and springs which were the basis of the community prosperity were the property of the Crown, despite their being open to one and all for use. If the land was to be parcelled up and sold the wells would no longer be available, and all the innkeepers, hoteliers, shopkeepers, farmers and general labourers would be deprived of their livings. There would also be nothing to stop the new owners either closing the wells or exploiting them on their own terms.

It would have been easy for the townspeople to have done nothing, other than perhaps to moan and blame their misfortune on someone else. Fortunately, however, that sense of destiny and will to survive which always manages to triumph at critical moments in the town's history asserted itself. Representations were made to Parliament, and an agreement was reached whereby a number of commissioners would survey the area and designate 200 acres of land which would link up all the then known mineral springs and which would:

'... for ever hereafter remain open and unenclosed, and all persons whomsoever shall and may have free access at all times to the said springs, and be at liberty to use and drink the Waters there arising, and take the benefit thereof, and shall and may have use, and enjoy full and free ingress, egress and regress in, upon, and over the said two hundred acres of land, and every part thereof ...'

The commissioners made their Award in 1778. Thus the Harrogate Stray came into being. The framework of modern Harrogate was then established: two ancient villages of High and Low Harrogate; the Stray, which curved round like a great horseshoe linking up the villages by means of a route which followed the lines of the new turnpike roads and the location of important mineral wells such as the Tewit and St John's Well; and – of great import for the future – the huge area of agricultural land between the two villages.

The guarantee of continuity provided by the Award of 1778 acted as a stimulus to growth. The crowds in attendance at the wells and public rooms of the inns were a colourful lot. Along with the aristocracy and their large retinues could be found the social climbers, tricksters, charlatans, quacks, salvationist preachers, invalids, traders and – keeping a sharp eye on all – the innkeepers, who as ever were concerned to maintain their positions by ensuring that their facilities and services met the expectations of all their guests. All their paying guests, that is. It was to this motley gathering that the racing fraternity flocked when a

St John's Chapel of 1749 was succeeded by Christ Church in 1831, which still lies at the heart of High Harrogate.

The Old Parsonage on Park Parade.

Mansfield House, Harrogate's most perfect Georgian building, was built as a theatre in 1788 directly opposite the Granby. It is now a private house.

racecourse was laid out (somewhat arbitrarily and probably in breach of the 1778 Award) on High Harrogate Stray by Colonel Clement Wolsley in 1793, it being a mile and a half in circumference and sixteen yards wide.

A further sign of Georgian Harrogate's boom years was the decision of Mrs Wilks at the Granby Hotel to replace makeshift Granby Barn Theatre with a new custom-built structure. This was done with Samuel Butler's 'circuit troop' in mind, which moved between Harrogate and Richmond during the 'season'. In 1789 the circuit was extended to Kendal, with Ripon following in 1792, Northallerton in 1800 and Beverley in 1808. The peak of the season was of course reserved for Harrogate, when from the 10th July until the 22nd September, performances would be given in the splendid new structure erected in Church Square directly opposite the Granby in 1788.

Ticket costs were extremely high. The cheapest gallery seats cost one shilling, the pit being double this rate, and boxes treble. The practice of the day was to sell tickets in advance, but not to assign places until the doors opened. Ticket holders were therefore in the habit of sending their servants to keep seats for them. Patronage from noble visitors or one of the great hotels was not uncommon and the playbill would then be headed with the phrase, 'By desire of the Most Noble the Marquis of Ely', or 'By particular desire of Lady Massey', and so on.

Programmes were extremely varied. Farquhar's restoration comedy *The Beaux Stratagem* was performed 'By desire of the Countess of Milltown' on the 6th July 1790. Knowing the power of the local landlords, how the audience must have relished landlord Bonniface's lines: 'As for fish, truly Sir, we are an inland town, and indifferently provided with fish, that's the truth on't.' The shortage of fish had long been a contentious point in Harrogate, and although a 'fish machine' passed from Stockton to Leeds via Harrogate every Wednesday, the supply was snapped up by the biggest hotels, leaving nothing for humbler establishments.

Harrogate Theatre presented scenes of the utmost animation, both inside and outside, at the approach of the nineteenth century. Outside, the muddy footpaths across the Stray from the Granby, the Queen and the Dragon, as well as from Low Harrogate, were filled with visitors, some on foot and others in sedan chairs. The correspondence between Lord Auckland and Alexander Wedderburn records an example of what must have been a regular occurrence when two sedan chairs vying for the dryest part of the footpath collided, causing the carriers to start an unseemly brawl, egged on by the near-apopleptic occupants, one of whom ended up in the mud. Carriages and a regular stream of horses also reached the theatre, depositing their passengers before its portals, around which the local rustics would be waiting together with the inevitable shady characters and ladies whose virtue may not have been as white as a Woods of Harrogate bleached linen bed-sheet. Torch-bearers and runners were also present during the hours of darkness, for the district was by no means clear of the pestilential highwayman and cut-purse, as the *Leeds Mercury* records.

One of the most regular visitors to Harrogate Theatre was the Lord Chancellor Alexander Wedderburn, first Baron Loughborough from 1780 and first Earl of Rosslyn from 1801. After having acquired land in Harrogate in 1775, he went on to build Wedderburn House (completed in 1786) and at the same time he generously erected a stone pump room over the neighbouring St John's Well, discovered back in 1631. His mansion lay but a few minutes drive to the south of the theatre at the end of a carriage road which crossed the Stray.

Wedderburn had a real interest in the theatre, only natural in a man of such cultivation and ability. As a friend of both Garrick and Sheridan, he was certainly in an ideal position to keep informed of current developments in English drama. But at a more homely level he also encouraged local talent. One such was Tryphosa Jane Wallis, who was seen by the Wedderburns at the first Harrogate Theatre in 1785, and given such encouragement as to allow her a successful career on the stage.

At the other end of the social ladder, opposite to the world of nobility and exclusive hotels, existed that of the poor classes, whose government was the responsibility of the parish, or in the case of Harrogate, the twin parishes of Pannal and Bilton-

Alexander Wedderburn, the first Earl of Rosslyn and Lord Chancellor. His Harrogate mansion was conveniently placed between London and Edinburgh.

with-Harrogate. The traditional mechanism of such government was the vestry meeting, with powers to appoint officers for collection of the poor rate and the highways rate, and for the adminstration of rudimentary services for policing and the Poor Law. The parishes also had responsibility for enforcing militia requirements. Certainly the propensity of the citizens of Harrogate for quarrelling among themselves was no less in the past than it is in the present. Constable Henry Bentley recorded in his accounts for 1675: 'ffor going twice to Sulphur Well to cease quarrells: £0.1.0.' That these disputes took place between the lower orders is not to be doubted, as the upper orders structured their quarrels in more formal manner, usually by means of the duel or the law suit.

The dawn of a new century also saw a change in the public demand for Harrogate water. Hitherto, the chalybeate springs of High Harrogate had been supreme in the general estimation. But, probably as a result of the greater need for warm water therapy to treat the victims of the French Wars, a fashion for bathing in heated sulphur water was spreading. The Old Sulphur Well in Low Harrogate, which Celia Fiennes described in 1697 as being 'so very strong and offensive that I could not force my horse near', now came into its own.

The manner of bathing at Harrogate does not appear to have changed much between the earliest recorded bathing establishment being opened in High Harrogate in around 1663 by Dr Neale and that of 1810. A wooden tub was filled with water heated from a large copper, previously extracted from the public wells and brought to the bathing establishment in barrels. According to the dictates of medical supervision, the victim was required to be submerged in this steaming hell for the prescribed period, before being hauled out and wrapped in blankets (which themselves had been used by dozens of previous sufferers) to 'sweat'. Tobias Smollett has left a highly descriptive account in his novel *Humphry Clinker*, which clearly owes much to his visit of May 1766:

'Harrogate water, so celebrated for its efficacy in the scurvy and other distempers, is supplied from a copious spring, in the hollow of a wild common, round which a good many houses have been built for the convenience of the drinkers. . . . The lodgers of each Inn form a distinct society that eat together; and there is a commodious public room where they breakfast in dishabille, at separate tables from 8 o'clock till eleven . . . here also they drink tea in the afternoon,

The astute Tobias Smollett used his Harrogate experience of 1766 to devastating effect in his novel Humphry Clinker.

and play cards or dance in the evening ... there is a public ball by subscription every night at one of the houses, to which all the company from the others are admitted by tickets; and indeed Harrogate treads on the heels of Bath, in the articles of gaiety and dissipation – with this difference, however, that here we are more sociable and familiar. One of the Inns is already full up to the very garretts, having no less than fifty lodgers, and as many servants. ...

As for the water, which is said to have effected so many surprising cures, I have drank it once, and the first draft has cured me of all desire to repeat the medicine. Some people say it smells of rotten eggs, and others compare it to the scourings of a foul gun. . . . I was obliged to hold my nose with one hand while I advanced the glass to my mouth with the other; and after I had made shift to swallow it, my stomach could hardly retain what it had received. The only effects it produced were sickness, griping and insurmountable disgust. I can hardly mention it without puking . . . Mr Micklewhimmen recommended a hot bath of these waters so earnestly, that I was over-persuaded to try the experiment. He had used it often with success, and always stayed an hour in the bath, which was a tub filled with Harrowgate water, heated for the purpose. If I could hardly bear the smell of a single tumbler when cold, you may guess how my nose was regailed by the steams arising from a hot bath of the same fluid. At night I was conducted into a dark hole on the ground floor, where the tub smoked and stunk like the pot of Acheron in one corner, and in another stood a dirty bed provided with thick blankets, in which I was to sweat after coming out of the bath. My heart seemed to die within me when I entered this dismal bagnio, and found my brain assaulted by such insufferable effluvia. I cursed Micklewhimmen for not considering that my organs were forged on this side of the Tweed; but being ashamed to recoil upon the threshold, I submitted to the process.

After having endured all but real suffocation for above a quarter of an hour in the tub, I was moved to the bed, and wrapped in blankets. There I lay a full hour panting with intolerable heat, but not the least moisture appearing upon my skin. I was carried to my chamber, and passed the night without closing an eye, in such a flutter of spirits as rendered me the most miserable wretch in being. I should certainly have run distracted, if the rarefaction of my blood, occasioned by that Stygian bath, had not burst the vessels, and produced a violent hemorrhage, which though

Hale's Bar – originally the Promenade Inn – would have been known to Smollett during his visit of 1766.

dreadful and alarming, removed the horrible disquiet. I lost two pounds of blood and more, on this occasion, and find myself still weak and languid: but, I believe, a little exercise will forward my recovery. . . .'

Despite such uncomplimentary accounts as this, the use of hot sulphur baths was greatly outstripping consumption of chalybeate water by 1800. As a sign of this, the growing awareness by the citizens of the need for improved amenities produced those amenities at Low Harrogate only, in the immediate neighbourhood of the Old Sulphur Well and the Crown Hotel. Dr Caley, with approval and support from the innkeepers, set up a subscription in 1804 to raise money to pay for a public assembly room. This was the only method of financing improvements, other than for an individual to support the entire cost from his own pocket, as happened with Alexander Wedderburn and the St John's Well pump room. (In other words, if you wanted something done, you had to do it yourself – no whining to the council about how to spend other people's money.) The assembly room idea took root, and subscriptions flowed in. Nor is this surprising in retrospect. No matter how luxuriously appointed the great inns and hotels were, no matter how many amenities were provided, they remained nevertheless open only to those who were guests and therefore of restricted social opportunity. A public assembly room would provide all the visitors with a means of mixing. On a more severely practical front, it would also afford protection near to the Old Sulphur Well from the worst of the weather.

Work on the new assembly room, to be known as the Promenade, continued throughout 1805, and was followed with great interest by the editor of the *Leeds Mercury* who wrote on the 24th May 1806 that:

'... we understand that the Promenade, now being erected at Harrogate, is nearly finished, and will be opened on 16th June with some select pieces of music on the organ. This elegant and commanding building stands in the middle of a garden and is intended as a Morning Lounge for the Company who will assemble every morning at the Wells.'

The Promenade Room is today the Mercer Gallery.

The opening of the Promenade Room brought one project to a successful conclusion, and the citizens immediately set about planning another. The Old Sulphur Well was open to all – bad weather included. The suggestion was floated that a cover would be useful to protect drinkers from rain, wind and cold.

The original Assembly Room, built in 1805–6, and now the Mercer Art Gallery.

Georgian elegance overlooking the Stray at High Harrogate.

Well Hill in 1772, showing the stone well-heads which survive beneath the Royal Pump Room.

However, a fully protective structure would infringe the Award of 1778 which required the wells to be open. A solution was found by designing a Roman temple which could shelter the well, pump and drinkers, and yet stay within the requirements of the Award by means of Tuscan columns instead of enclosing walls.

A public subscription raised £231.12.0. and a design from Thomas Chippendale was approved. A date for opening was fixed for the 5th April 1808. Then, the committee started to look for a builder. This sequence is of interest. Having raised money, decided the design and settled upon an opening date, the committee left the matter of the builder until last, on the principle that

16

Well Hill in 1820, showing the temple built by public subscription in 1807–8.

the customer should dictate the terms. None of your modern nonsense about inflation costs, construction difficulties, or making allowances for design alterations or labour problems. The project was completed on time. Low Harrogate was taking on an appearance to rival High Harrogate.

The population of Harrogate in 1810 was about 1,500, which represented an increase of some fifty per cent since 1800, an incredible growth rate in any terms. Since 1801 there had been calls for the construction of a workhouse to house the homeless paupers of the area, although the choice of a site was never agreed. Eventually, and after much dispute, a workhouse was opened in 1810 at a site as far away from aristocratic

17

High Harrogate and rapidly expanding Low Harrogate as possible – right at the bottom of the hill which led to Starbeck. Before this time the parish had sent its paupers to Pannal Workhouse where, for a fee, Harrogate was rid of them. After 1810 all that changed and Harrogate was in a position to take paupers from other townships – again, for a fee.

The great majority of visitors probably saw nothing more disagreeable than the invalids drinking at the wells. The years between 1810 and the coming of the railways in 1848 were the climax of a particular style of spa life which would be irretrievably lost at the advent of greater opportunities for mass popular transportation. A wonderful account of Harrogate during these years was written by Henry Curling, which is worth reproducing in full:

The Harrogate Workhouse (never fashionable) was built in 1810.

WHAT scenes of life have we not beheld at Harrowgate! what days of romance, and nights of revelry and excitement, have we not passed at the far-famed Dragon, even a quarter of a century back, when on that bare, Scotchified looking common, were assembled, in the huge stone-built halls, with their terraces and gardens, which constituted the hotels of the place, half the fashion and beauty of the kingdom; where the great sporting men of the day met; where mothers trotted out their daughters in all their charms, and country squires (who had mentally resolved to be unconnubial) learnt the trick of wiving; where fortunes were won by the turn-up of a card by old dowagers, whilst their "radiant and exquisite daughters" lost their hearts to some lord of sash and epaulette in the dance.

The Dragon at Harrowgate (in those days) was unlike any other *table d'hôte* of the time; it was more like some nobleman's seat, where the *élite* of the world of fashion had been invited to spend the summer months. A constant succession of guests

Well Hill, with relics of times when Low Harrogate was but a village on the moors.

were continually arriving and departing; and there were personages whose names were familiar amongst the aristocracy of the land, and where, consequently, in place of the pinched and crabbed manners of the present day, were to be found hearty old English manners, sociality, good feeling, and jollity.

But few perhaps of the present generation can recollect Harrowgate much before the period we are writing of, though, doubtless, there are some old stagers who can remember those choice and master spirits of the place who were wont to keep the table in a roar, when old Goodlad was host of the Green Dragon, during whose administration it was almost as impossible for a parvenu, or a party without four horses and liveried attendants to match, to gain a footing at the hotel, as at that time it would have been for himself to become member for a close borough.

At the Dragon in those days there was generally some prima donna who led the *ton*, some queen-bee of the hive who ruled the roast (if we may so term it), a sort of lady-patroness of high rank; to offend whom would be to subject oneself to be cashiered by the gay assemblage. Her glance of approval or rejection would, indeed, be certain either to sanction the introduction of a new-comer into the *crême de la crême* of the circle, or keep them at so uncomfortable a distance, that they would be frozen into the necessity of seeking the warmer climates of either of the other houses on the neighbouring common.

If we are writing our annals truly, and memory does not fail us, there were, in our time, four hotels at this celebrated watering-place, namely, The Dragon, The Granby, The Queen's Head, and The Crown. These houses bore the several nicknames of The House of Commons, The House of Lords, The Hospital, and the Manchester Warehouse. The

The White Hart was the scene of a spectacular Waterloo Ball in 1815 when 'An unusual assemblage of beauty and fashion graced the rooms ... after partaking of an elegant supper, separated at 2.00 o'clock in the morning, highly delighted with the evening's entertainments'.

Bilton House, one of the many aristocratic residences built in High Harrogate.

The boyhood home of the great Victorian painter W P Frith, now the site of Mornington Crescent.

Granby (which stood upon the heath towards the pleasant town of Knaresborough), and which, with its fine shrubberies and pleasant gardens, looked like some Yorkshire hall, was called The House of Lords. There the most staid and straight-laced, and the invalided portions of the aristocracy resorted. The Dragon, again, which stands in the Ripon Road, just at one end of the common, pleasantly situated, with its garden and terrace, amongst the verdant fields, was yclept The House of Commons. There the sporting gentry of the day, the great turf men, mixed up with a sprinkling of the aristocracy, and the old country families, together with parties from the north: Highland lairds, and rollicking blades from the Emerald Isle, met together year after year, and kept up one continued revel during the season; the assemblage being, almost without exception, formed of people of condition, and character in the island.

The Crown was called The Hospital, and was situated in what constituted the town of Low Harrowgate. In appearance it was not unlike a receptacle for the sick, and was erected close beside a well of the most fœtid and foul-smelling water. This house was usually the resort of the water-drinking portion of the visitors, folks whose Bardolphic visages had caused a trial of this nauseous puddle to be recommended by the faculty. The Queen's Head was a long, irregular built Scotch-looking mansion, standing also upon the edge of the common, almost opposite The Granby; and, sheltered by a few tall trees, looked the diamond of the desert. This again was denominated The Manchester Warehouse, and was mostly tenanted by the trading portion of the company; the great Manchester millocrat, the rich pinmaker from Birmingham, the wealthy cutler from Sheffield, the iron-founder from Black Barnsley, the clothier from Leeds, and the moneyed man from Glasgow, Dundee, and Paisley; folks who dared not, at that period, attempt admission either into the Dragon or Granby, and who were hardly sufficiently assured in their position to venture even amongst the jewels of the Crown.

The Dragon was the house for those who came to seek for pleasure and amusement. Amongst the other diversions got up to beguile time, high play was constantly resorted to, and the card-room was usually filled with players at this period, with very little intermission during the twenty-four hours. There they sat—that infatuated and devoted clique—hour after hour in a recess to the right of the long room, which was called the "Tea-room." Some dozen tables were filled with the oddest of all the oddities of the play-men of the turf, the most celebrated sporting characters of that day, and perhaps the most determined amongst the gentlemen gamblers in England. They were also surrounded and attended, during their orgies, by a whole fraternity of betters,—men who, with cat-like watch, hovered over and flitted from table to table computing the chances, and calculating the odds of the different games.

So absorbed were some of the sporting part of the company in this vice, that we have known men pass a whole season in the card-room, with slight intermission, seated at those tables, morning, noon, and night. Whist constituted their world; and their utmost idea of happiness on this side the grave, consisted in four by honours and the odd trick. One or two of these devotees we remember, with parchment visage, and "lack-lustre eye," who would scarce give themselves time to eat, allowing but little for repose, and none for exercise. These persons would jump up at the sound of the dressing bell, make a hasty toilet, rush down stairs again, and even win or lose large sums in the short space of time before the bell again sounded for dinner. Whilst at table they would bolt their meals in a state of feverish excitement, consequent upon their gaming propensities, make sundry high bets over their port and claret; and then, again, when the tables were drawn, they would rush to the card-room, and, spending the watches of the night in play, refuse to move till the serving-maids of the establishment, coming down to set the apartments in order, forced them to their pillows.

We remember a lady of rank, who, after a life spent at the card-table, died with the pack in her hand. As regularly as the season came round, she drove to the Dragon with her lovely daughters, desired the postilion, after setting down herself and imperials, to take the young ladies into a boarding-school; after which, returning the bow of the obsequious host, and shaking hands with the various parties she was acquainted with, she would walk straight into the card-room, cut in, and commence play.

We also knew a devoted son of the clergy, one of the finest preachers of the day, who was wont to treat his congregation with a sermon during morning service, upon the enormity of gaming; after which, he would ascend his curricle, drive to the Dragon, and pass the entire remainder of the sabbath behind the closed blinds of the card-room, absorbed body and soul in whist, or setting the fee-simple of his living upon a turn of the dice-box.

We recollect a rich Indian nabob, who successively lost three fortunes at Harrowgate, Cheltenham, and Buxton.

It was, however, highly amusing (at this period) to take an occasional glance at the countenances of these devotees, and watch the ebb and flow of their several fortunes. Lady ——, who, I have before said, died at the card-table, would at times have her lap filled with banknotes, which she had no leisure to count. This lady was wont to play frequently for a cool hundred a game, and at the same time bet with those near her table. Nay, we have heard, that on one occasion she continued playing two whole nights and days at piquet with a German noble, to whom she lost a large sum, when quitting the tables to join the company assembled at supper, after a ball, she nearly fainted from exhaustion and chagrin.

Quietly, and with determined perseverance, would the devoted slaves of this absorbing vice continue their incessant cutting, dealing, shuffling, and playing. Hour after hour through the day were the sun's rays excluded from their pallid features, and hour after hour, during the night, they pursued the same employment. The orchestra brayed out its joyous strains unheard or unmarked—the merry dance was kept up in the Tea-room, beside which they played—the waltz was ended, the supper over—and still, diamonds, hearts, spades, and clubs, seemed to afford renewed interest every moment.

Harrowgate, like many other watering places, has fallen away. It was in our nonage that we used to visit it in its palmy state; during the chequered light of maturer years we have lost sight of that and other places of amusement. But once, we returned to this place after a long interval, and it seemed that we met the ghosts of our departed joys. A new race had sprung up,—mirth and jollity seemed banished. The roar of mirth no longer was heard at the tables. The card-room was deserted,—the billiard-rooms were empty; and although there seemed a decent sprinkling of guests at the hotels, compared with the choice and master spirits of former times, the assemblage was a quakers' meeting: they appeared "to have lost all mirth, and foregone all custom or exercise." It is indeed, as Mrs. Trollope observes, always *the who*, and not *the where* that makes the difference of enjoyments in a public place. The waters smelt as villanously as ever; the heather bloomed upon the common, where stood the

West Park developed after 1800 and grew along to the crossroads where the Brunswick Inn was established.

various inns, but the spirit of the place seemed gone with its former visitors; the pegs had slipped, the music ceased, and Harrowgate (as a place of amusement) was naught.

Lord Byron, a visitor to Harrogate in 1806 when he stayed at the Crown.

In former days, the road before the terrace of the Dragon presented a most animated scene, being filled, after breakfast, with gay equipages—fours-in-hand, curricles, and tandems; whilst whole bevies of ladies and attendant cavaliers were to be seen mounting their palfreys, to excursionize to the various places of interest in the neighbourhood; added to which, there was always some device or divertissement got up by the master of the revels, to pass away the long age between the morning meal and the dinner hour. At one part of the season, races were held upon the common, and if the running was not quite so good as at Newmarket or Doncaster, the fun was greater: the genteel attendance and elegant equipages on the course, made the scene gay and animated in the extreme. Most of the visitors at the different hotels were wont to drive to the heath, on such occasions; besides which, many of the gentry living around, made a point of frequenting these races. Almost all were known to each other, and the lone common, with its Scotchified belt of pines on one side, and the extensive and well-wooded view on the other, appeared like the scene in Scott's "Old Mortality," when Lady Margaret Bellenden and her party attended at the Wappershaw. Rural sports for the amusement of the more rustic gathering, were also carried on with some spirit after the races, and between the heats. Bumpkins were to be seen chasing pigs with soaped tails at one part, while strapping wenches ran a well contested race for a chemisette; after which, rough-headed louts clambered up a greased pole for the leg of mutton which bid defiance to their efforts at its top. Then there were jingling matches, in which some nineteen fellows, being blindfolded, were started to catch the twentieth, whose eyes were uncovered, and who was accommodated with a sheep-bell tied between his legs. Men also were bribed to plunge their heads for half-crowns in tubs of water, till they were half-drowned, and subsequently to dive into bags of flour and grope for shillings, till they were half-choked. Besides there were many other rural sports and diversions, since refined away, voted vulgar, and forgotten.

We remember many specimens of the English Esquire of the old school too, who used to visit this watering place every season,—gentlemen with manners as peculiar to their day, and as refined, as their costume of a former century was quaint and characteristic—gentlemen of the Grandison school, who would keep their hats in the air whilst addressing a lady; and conduct her into a room, not tucked under one arm like a country lass at a hop, but hand in hand, as if just about to lead off in the *minuet de la cour*,—gentlemen, who would no more think of sitting down to dinner without donning their ribbed silks, than they would be likely to appear at breakfast out of their buck-skins, buckled tops, quaint-cut blue coats, pomatummed side locks, and well tied pig-tails.

Others again there were, rough, eccentric humourists, hearty old bucks, rough and ready as Squire Western himself, and speaking in a dialect as provincial as the clodpoles on their estates,—characters now no longer to be met with, and who seemed the last of their race. There were also several varieties of the Buck Parson, with here and there a representative of the Old Soldier of half a century previous to the Peninsular triumphs,—warriors who were majors on full pay when they cried for more pap "in the nurses' arms," and who were wont to set their squadrons in the field when the most arduous duties of the dragoon officer consisted in carrying three and four bottles beneath his belt nightly, with a proper and dignified deportment.

Many of the great sporting characters of the day also had seats in the vicinity of Harrowgate. These gentlemen would often drive over, mix in the amusements of the company, and carry off their friends to their homes. The great sportsman of his day (Thornton) brought his hawks upon one occasion, and flew them upon the common; after which he invited the assemblage to return with him to Thornville Royal, and entertained them with a degree of splendour not often seen in those days.

The Colonel, indeed, lived in a style of almost regal magnificence at that period; his hawks, hounds, and stud have perhaps never been equalled before or since. He was the wittiest man of his day, too; no table at which he sat but was in a roar from beginning to end of the feast, and his hospitality was exercised in a style peculiar to himself and his generous spirit; magnums of port and claret, holding a dozen bottles each, graced the festive board, and a loving cup revolved around, containing a dozen of champagne in its capacious depths. On these occasions there was no lack of amusement; the Colonel's voice made the halls echo to the hunter's cry, and as "his eye begot occasion for his wit," his joyous spirit turned everything to mirth. The very spirit of fun twinkled in his laughing visage. He seemed as if he could have "jested in an hospital, and moved wild laughter in the throat of death." Perhaps some of our readers may, even yet, remember the circumstances of the great sportsman's removal from his hunting grounds at Faulknor's Hall, upon the Wolds of Yorkshire, to his seat in Wiltshire, when he made a progress through the land like some cavalier of olden times upon the march. First came the huntsmen, whippers-in, and grooms with various packs of dogs, as celebrated in that county as the hounds of Theseus; next walked the falconers in their green attire, carrying the hawks hooded upon their frames; after them marched the trainers with a whole squadron of thorough-breds, racers, hunters, and hackneys; then followed the greyhounds in their cloths—that famous breed whose portraits are still to be seen—boat carriages, and equipages of every sort, together with terriers, water-dogs and spaniels, accompanied by innumerable serving-men, dog-carts, and baggage-waggons bringing up the rear. We might indeed supply a volume of picturesque scenes in which the gay Colonel with his green hat, and his partridge-coloured coat, was an actor at Harrowgate; but the above must suffice.

The personages thus described reached Harrogate either in their own splendid carriages or in the great stagecoaches which were such a vital part of life in old England before the railways. Most of the town's hotels and inns were coaching inns, being stops on the routes of the coaches passing through Harrogate. A few, such as the lordly Granby, were fully-blown posting houses with stand for thirty carriages and stabling for a hundred horses. At these posting houses, coaches were not only serviced and teams exchanged but fresh carriages and postillions could be hired. The arrival of one of the Harrogate stages – such as the splendidly-named Rocket, Dart, True Briton, Tally-Ho, or Teazle – must have been a sight to quicken the pulse of the most seasoned spa visitor.

This beautiful Regency terrace gave its name to Brunswick Station, opened in 1848 on the land opposite the present Prince of Wales Mansions.

High Harrogate's principal street, now called Park Parade and Regent Parade, developed as a row of lodging houses and shops in the eighteenth century.

When Jonathan Benn retired from the Granby he built this villa, calling it St Albans in grateful recognition for the value of business brought to him by the patronage of the Duchess of St Albans.

The George Inn, most conveniently sited on the Ripon turnpike road, has extended over the centuries to its present palatial size. The great actor Macready stayed here in 1833.

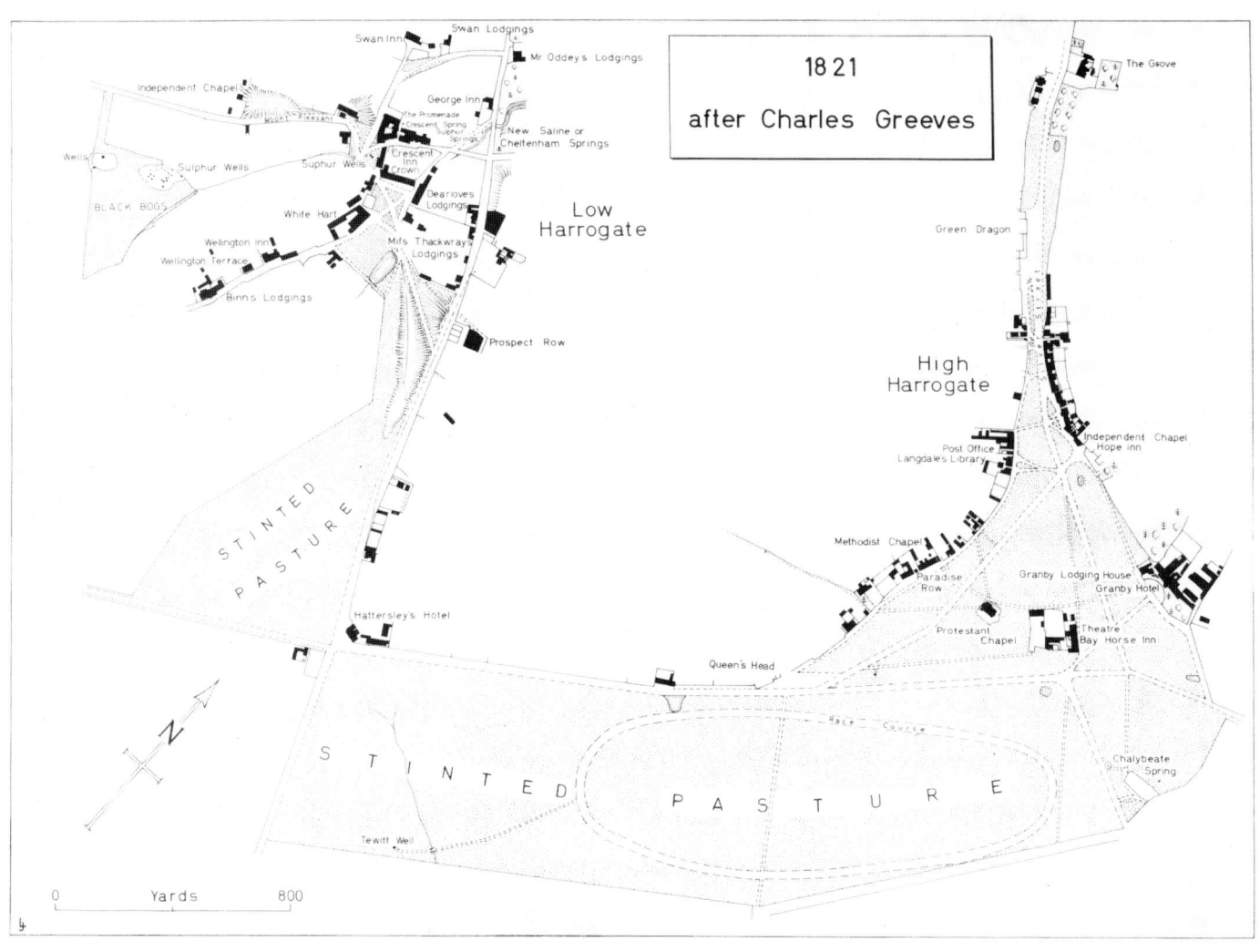

The two villages of High and Low Harrogate in 1821.

Along the turnpike roads which bisected the noble greensward of the Stray, the grinding, rolling team of coach and horses would move, all groaning wood, creaking leather, jingling brass, steaming horses and impatient passengers, accompanied no doubt by a crowd of urchins taking good care to keep out of reach of the coachman's whip and the turning wheels of the great vehicle. And in the stable yard, where word of

The Victoria Baths in Crescent Gardens.

impending arrival had gone before, a sudden stirring as ostlers, grooms, post-boys, baggage servants and others hurried to their positions. The great and famous would certainly have been received in person by the innkeepers and hoteliers, by Benn of the Granby, Goodlad – and later Frith – of the Dragon, Dearlove of the Queen and Thackwray of the Crown. By such means arrived the princes and the dukes, the earls and the countesses, when "the Right Honorables, the MP's, the Baronets and their ladies pour into Harrogate, chase away all the vulgar before them . . . and fill the Granby with "Ha-ha's" and "How-do's"'.

The glorious development continued throughout the following decades. Hotel outbid hotel in efforts to improve standards: more musicians for the soirées; a greater variety of delicacies for the table than last year; celebrated entertainers for the long rooms and the theatre never before obtained – but of course.

A change of emphasis occurred when entrepreneur John Williams arrived in Harrogate in the 1830's. Realising that existing provisions for bathing were grossly inadequate and that there was an opportunity for imaginative speculation, he obtained land directly behind the fashionable Promenade Room and constructed the Victoria Baths to a design by Leeds architect, Clarke. The building was a long, low structure in severely classical style, with Ionic columns and dominant window frames, and its arrival proved immensely influential on the future architectural development of the town.

Mr Thackwray's Montpellier Baths.

The new Victoria Baths were a great success, both financially and as an amenity for the visitors. The message was not lost on the hoteliers of Low Harrogate, one of whom immediately prepared plans of his own. The Thackwray family had owned the Crown Hotel at least from 1740, when Joseph Thackwray 'came to the Crown'. His descendant at the Crown, also called Joseph, was a man of great ability, being ambitious, hard-working, ruthless, stubborn, and generous. In fact, an amalgam of all those qualities typical of the successful Victorian man of business. The Crown Hotel estate at this time reached from its present area right up the hill to Parliament Street, most of which land was set out as a garden or 'pleasure ground'. On part of this land, Mr Thackwray erected a suite of baths to rival the Victoria Baths, and as if to stress this ensured that the Greek revival style of architecture was employed. The

Harrogate's most perfect building, the Spa Rooms of 1835, seen in this early photograph of about 1860.

Montpellier or Crown Baths were opened in 1834 just two years after Williams' Victoria Baths. They, too, were a huge success and provided luxurious standards for bathing under medical supervision never before seen in the town.

Private enterprise was the making of early Victorian Harrogate. Having been so clearly eclipsed by Mr Thackwray, Mr Williams decided to go one better. Just across the Stray from his Victoria Baths on the eastern side of Ripon Road, a series of important mineral springs had been discovered in 1818 which, because of their similarity to the famous spring at Cheltenham, were called the 'Cheltenham Springs'. The discovery meant that Low Harrogate could not only provide all the important sulphur springs, including the world's strongest at the Old Sulphur Well, but a series of chalybeate springs, one of which was later identified as the world's strongest chloride of iron spring. Having

Cheltenham Pump Room, Harrogate, Yorkshire.

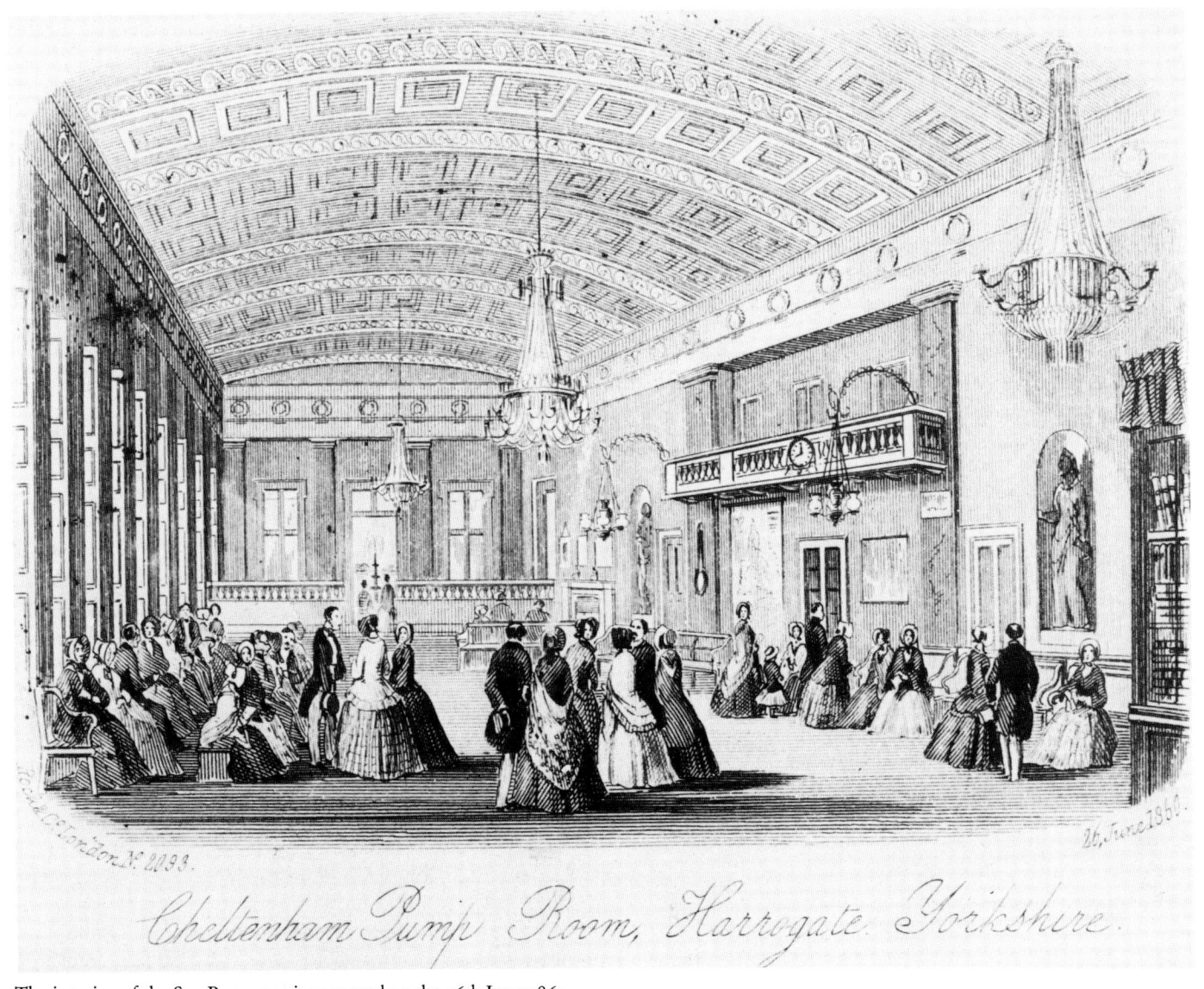

The interior of the Spa Rooms as it appeared on the 26th June 1860.
The musicians' gallery is on the right.

acquired the site, Mr Williams commissioned his architect Clarke to design a building to accommodate, not only a pump and drinking area, but a great new assembly room. Everything was to be on the grandest scale, with the very highest quality of workmanship.

Clarke's design was a masterpiece. The new building was in the shape of a Greek temple, with a mighty portico in pure Doric style facing Ripon Road. Internally, areas were provided for the pump, and a large assembly hall with musicians' gallery, the whole crowned with a beautifully coffered ceiling.

The grand opening occurred on Friday the 21st August 1835, with a public ball which was unquestionably the most brilliant social event ever to have taken place at Harrogate outside the exclusive hotels. After a series of preliminary events organised by the committee formed by their Royal Highnesses Lord and Lady Blayney, Major Massov, Dr Dorratt and Captains Frobisher and McDowall, the grand ball started at 9.00pm. The whole estate was brilliantly illuminated that evening, and the climax of the ball came with the arrival of the fabulously wealthy Duke of St Albans, whose stepdaughter became strongly attached to Harrogate. The following day saw festivities, including a firework display and continuing performances by the Band of the Scots Greys.

With the completion of the Cheltenham Spa Rooms – as the building was for a time called – Harrogate had received what was unquestionably the most magnificent structure ever to be erected within its boundary. The Spa Rooms building represented the climax of the classical style in Harrogate, and influenced the development of the town's architecture for a century to come.

At the same time as the spectacular developments just described were going on, other forces, less obviously grand, were at work. The Award of 1778 had allocated large areas of land in Harrogate to such families as the Ingilbys of Ripley or the Thackwrays.

At the same time, great quantities were reserved for the Crown by right of the Duchy of Lancaster. The 1820's and 1830's saw a developing interest by the duchy of its Harrogate estates, and it is no exaggeration to state that Harrogate owes its well-regulated townscape and high quality of building to the strict but benign control exercised by the duchy. To this day, the vast majority of people in Harrogate have little idea of the role of the Duchy of Lancaster in the successful growth of their town. Yet it is demonstrably true that the duchy has been the single greatest force working for the good of Harrogate throughout its history.

The innkeepers and hoteliers had supported a noble scheme to provide a hospital for the sick poor which could take advantage of the healing properties of the mineral springs. Meetings were held in 1818 and the movement gathered momentum. The Earl of Harewood gave land for the purpose, located directly opposite Bogs Field, and His Majesty King George IV headed the subscription with a gift of £52.10.0. The Royal Bath Hospital was completed in the spring of 1825, but a further period was required for the fitting-out. When the first patients were admitted, Harrogate had taken a major step along the road of hydrotherapeutic provision.

The great improvements effected during the 1820's and 1830's were not restricted to secular affairs. In Low Harrogate the lack of a church had for long meant that worshippers had been under the tiresome obligation of journeying to Pannal for divine service. In 1825, Low Harrogate Church, which later became known as St Mary's, was completed. Thanks to a gift of land from the Duchy of Lancaster and much work by the tireless Joseph Thackwray, Low Harrogate now had a church of its own, located on the Esplanade a few yards away from the junction with Cold Bath Road.

At High Harrogate the old Chapel of St John had become unsafe and grossly overcrowded, and a replacement church was clearly required. This was

Old St Mary's Church, Low Harrogate.

built in 1831 in a beautiful Early English style of architecture. As with St Mary's in Low Harrogate, the completion of Christ Church at High Harrogate owed much to the generosity and co-operation of the Duchy of Lancaster, not least over the important matter of a stipend for the clergyman. Details of the seating plans of the old Harrogate chapels and churches reveal that the majority of the best sittings were reserved for the innkeepers and hoteliers. At the new Christ Church, the Frith family of the Dragon Hotel were very much to the fore. Young W P Frith, who later achieved world fame as the painter of *Derby Day*, *Many Happy Returns* and *Ramsgate Sands*, would certainly have been familiar with the monuments and decorations of the new church.

The importance of the innkeepers and hoteliers, however, was at no time in greater evidence than during the decisive events which occurred in the winter following the opening of the Spa Rooms. For about twenty years the problem of vandalism at the wells had been growing. It had come to a crisis in 1821-2, when various groups of townspeople had sent

W P Frith, who long retained happy memories of his Harrogate boyhood.

petitions up to the duchy office asking for powers for the better protection of the wells. It was claimed that 'during the night time some persons unknown to your petitioners have put into the said Mineral Springs, quantities of Dung, Ashes, Dead Dogs and other animals of a most offensive nature. . . .' The first petition was opposed by another group who put proposals of their own to the duchy, who wisely suggested that a general improvement act might be preferable. This act was eventually passed in 1841 as the Harrogate Improvement Act, after the events of the winter of 1835.

Buildings at the Esplanade undertaken by the Duchy of Lancaster after 1840. E M Forster stayed in the hotel on the left in June 1910: 'I am going to Harrogate for a fortnight – a horrible and expensive experience, but my mother has been ordered there for the gout . . . they say the scenery is fine and the invalids genteel.'

Still presenting a domestic view, the view from the Old Swan in 1989.

On the morning of the 1st December 1835, the owner of the Swan Inn, Jonathan Shutt, left his establishment and walked along Swan Road towards the Old Sulphur Well, passing the shops which in those times backed onto the Crown Hotel and which belonged to Joseph Thackwray. One of these shops was tenanted by a man called Husband and was the nearest building to the public Old Sulphur Well. As Mr Shutt passed the entrance to the shop, he looked in and saw workmen digging a deep well. Thoroughly alarmed by this, Mr Shutt contacted the other leading citizens of the town, including Mr Benn of the Granby, Frith of the Dragon, Dearlove of the Queen and Williams of the Victoria Baths and Spa Rooms estate. The consensus was that Mr Thackwray was attempting to divert the waters of the valuable public

Promenade Terrace, built in the 1840's by Thomas Humble Walker between the Old Sulphur Well and the Swan Inn.

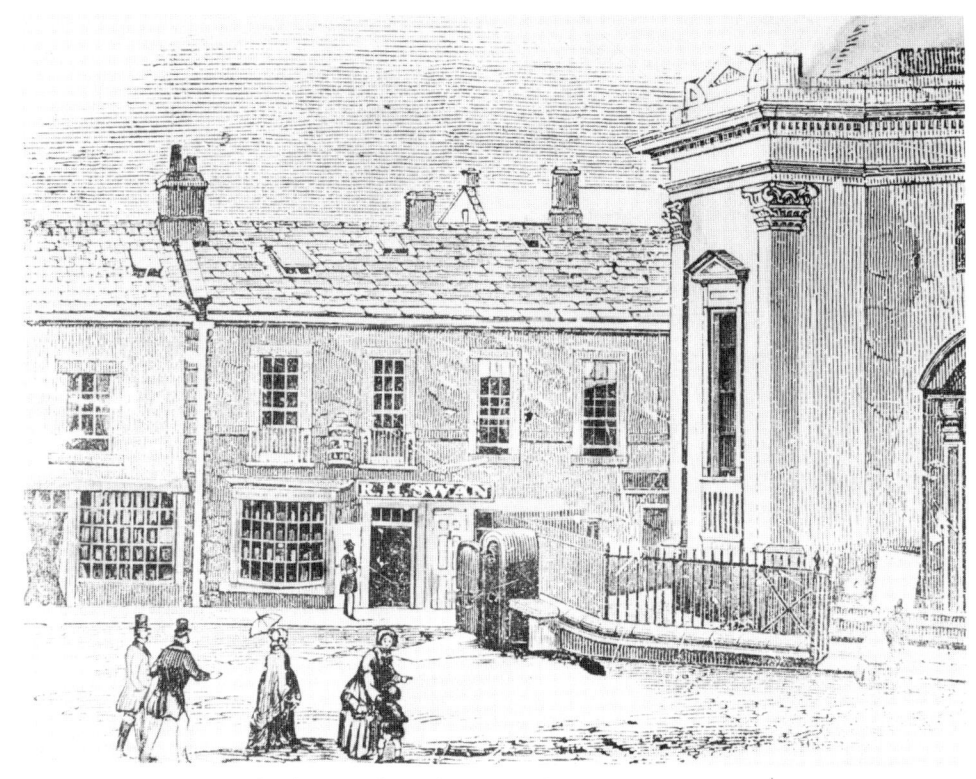

Husband's shop on the right next to the Pump Room was the site of Mr Thackwray's infamous attempt to divert the sulphur water from the public Old Sulphur Well in December 1835.

Sulphur Well into his own property in order to achieve a monopoly. He already controlled the rich supply on his Crown Hotel estate, and if he succeeded in putting the Old Sulphur Well out of action the only wells left for the public would be the few on the Stray.

Meetings were held in the Promenade Room and the senior citizens agreed to prosecute Thackwray, having already failed to persuade him to abandon his digging. After a long case which culminated in a trial at York Assizes, Mr Thackwray was acquitted on a technicality. For Harrogate, however, the shock had been severe. Public opinion was in the mood for action, and the supporters of new legislation had their way. With the full support of the Duchy of Lancaster, the Harrogate Improvement Bill was signed by Queen Victoria, and in 1841 the town elected twenty-one 'improvement commissioners' to govern and effect improvements by means of a limited power to rate. The Victorian age was now underway.

In keeping with a fine old tradition, the first thing the newly elected improvement commissioners did was to have a hell of a row. Having decided to build a

Isaac Thomas Shutt's Royal Pump Room of 1842 with the original dolphin crown still in place.

splendid new pump room over the Old Sulphur Well, they launched a competition for a design, which a majority decision awarded to the son of Jonathan Shutt, young Isaac Thomas. When news of this was made known, four of the most important commissioners (all from High Harrogate, be it noted) resigned on the spot. This came but a little while after the local 'what-ever-it-is-we're-against-it' society objected to the proposal to build a pump room on the grounds that such a construction would harm the waters!

Nevertheless, Isaac Thomas Shutt's Royal Pump Room was built, and opened to great acclaim on the 21st July 1842. From that day to this the octagonal, classical building has been regarded as the very symbol of Harrogate, and with some justification, for it was not only designed and built by local men, but the very stone of its fabric came from local quarries, designated by the Award of 1778. The cost of construction was covered by a unique rate, and additional income could be generated by means of an entrance fee. To provide for those who did not wish to pay but who preferred to

The Royal Pump Room, with (at left) the 1913 annex.

claim their legal right of free access to the waters, an outside tap was provided.

The completion of the Royal Pump Room marked the end of an era for the well women. These females were the 'spirits of the place', and earned a living by gathering water from the wells and providing glasses for its consumption. Although the water was of course free for all who desired it, only the bravest would have failed to tip she who proffered the service. Their appearance may not have changed much since Thomas Baskerville's description of them in 1675:

'Their faces did shine like bacon rind. And for beauty may vie with an old Bath guide's ass, the sulphur waters had so fouled their pristine complexions.'

The new Pump Room, with its vacuum pumps and

Trinity Church, overlooking land once occupied by Brunswick Station.

Betty Lupton, the 'Queen of the Well'.

Wedgewood tubes, removed the need for the well women. It is pleasant to record, however, that old Betty Lupton, the 'Queen of the Well', was permitted to work inside the new structure, and when she retired the following year in 1843 was accorded the unprecedented honour of a pension.

The 1841 Act contained clauses to enable the commissioners to provide a market, but the inhabitants were against the idea. Indeed, when the idea was first promulgated, a mob formed a procession with a discordant brass band at it head, followed by youths with dead cats and rotten eggs, and the prominent movers of the scheme were serenaded, hooted, bawled at and had their windows broken. The 'what-ever-it-is-we're-against-it' society won the day, just as five years previously when they had prosecuted the public-minded citizen who had donated seats for the Stray.

The idea of a market was in reality sensible, as it would have removed the nuisance of the street hawkers and barrow boys who perambulated goods round the town at the tail end of a donkey. Moreover, there was talk of a railway, which could bring produce quickly to the heart of the town. But in order to do this, it would have to cut into the sacred turf of the Stray!

The idea of bringing a railway to Harrogate was not generally liked. The innkeepers and hoteliers feared that it might lower the tone of the place and frighten away the aristocratic regulars. The columns of the recently established Harrogate newspapers were filled with foreboding that a railway would ruin the town, allowing the lower orders from Leeds and Bradford to flood into Harrogate, disturbing the peace. It was also feared that 'great Engines would frighten the grazing cattle' and that poorer visitors would bring their own food and (horrors!) walk about eating it.

The growth of the railway system in the 1840's was unstoppable. The first line to arrive was the York and

North Midland, which branched from Church Fenton via Wetherby. The Harrogate terminus at Brunswick Station, diagonally opposite the Brunswick Hotel on the corner of York Place and West Park, was reached by means of a tunnel beneath Langcliffe Avenue. It was opened to traffic on the 20th July 1848. Within the year the Leeds and Thirsk Company had opened a station at Starbeck, which was extended to York by 1862. Plans to link the Brunswick line with Starbeck by means of a central station were discussed, but in view of the insuperable problem of the Stray crossing the matter was dropped.

Of the many changes made possible by the railway, three things are outstanding. Firstly, it enabled more visitors to come to Harrogate. As the majority of these visitors were from the wealthy manufacturing classes of West Yorkshire and Lancashire, eager to experience the lifestyle of the aristocracy, the change was greatly to the advantage of the hoteliers. Secondly, the railway enabled a greater variety of consumer goods to be brought to Harrogate, which was good for trade and residents and visitors alike. Thirdly, it enabled the town's builders and developers to take advantage of the demand for property by importing large quantities of building materials. The railway stations were built of brick, and more and more developments included an element of this material – previously unknown in the stone-rich town.

If it is true to claim that before 1841, the hoteliers were the driving power in Harrogate, the advent of the elected improvement commissioners saw a shift. The new men were mostly self-made tradesmen with a desire to improve facilities other than those which would affect their own businesses. And some of them were gentlemen, with a wish to assist the growth of a promising community. Unfortunately, much of their early deliberations were occupied by ceaseless squabblings and useless litigation. The best of them was certainly Dr George Kennion, son of the Vicar of

Dr Kennion, greatest of the improvement commissioners until the era of Ellis.

Christ Church, who had been one of the first of the commissioners.

When gas lighting was introduced to the town in 1847 (amidst gloomy talk of unemployment among candle-makers), the commissioners began a long period of wrangling with the company over the price of gas. This grew to such a degree that the company subsequently cut off the supply, pitching the town into darkness. The chaos went on for months. In a memorable letter to the *Harrogate Advertiser* dated the 16th May 1849, Dr Kennion warned the townspeople of the folly of internal quarrels:

'Unless the inhabitants of Harrogate – whether of High Harrogate, or Low Harrogate – whether Commissioners or non-commissioners – unless all unite together, and throwing aside past differences and

Charles Dickens as he was at the time of his visit to Harrogate in 1858. His readings at the Spa Rooms were given before packed houses.

all littleness of mere party feeling – join together in furthering the real interests of Harrogate . . . this place, which is so favoured by nature, and which has so much in itself to attract the invalid, as well as the visitor who merely seeks for recreation, will gradually fall from being the most important watering-place of the north, to the position of the most insignificant of Spas . . . I have heard such remarks as the following: "Harrogate! who would go there that could help it? nothing done to make the place comfortable. The people are all too busy quarreling among themselves to have any time or attention to throw away upon visitors".'

His words were read by unresponsive minds.

Despite the unfortunate tendency described above, Harrogate prospered throughout the 1840's and 1850's. The visitors enjoyed the improved accessibility, the hotels were incomparable, the baths and treatments up-to-date and a greater variety of entertainments on offer than at any time in the past.

Literary celebrities were in regular attendance. Lord Byron had stayed at the Crown Hotel in 1806. In June 1827 the *Leeds Mercury* had reported that: 'The Harrogate Season has commenced very auspiciously this year, and the Lake Poets, Southey and Wordsworth, with their families, are now at this fashionable watering place.' When Charles Dickens came in September 1858 it was not as a visitor but as a businessman, and his public readings in the Spa Rooms appear to have been a great financial success. He thought that Harrogate was 'the queerest place, with the strangest people in it, leading the oddest lives of dancing, newspaper reading, and tables d'hote'. One of the audience in the Spa Rooms caught his attention:

'There was one gentleman at the Little Dombey [reading] yesterday who exhibited, or rather concealed, the profoundest grief. After crying a good deal without hiding it, he covered his face with both his hands and laid it down on the back of the seat before him and really shook with emotion. He was not in mourning, but I supposed him to have lost some child in old time. There was a remarkably good fellow of thirty or so, too, who found something so very ludicrous in "Toots", that he *could not* compose himself at all, but laughed until he sat wiping his eyes with his handkerchief, and whenever he felt "Toots" coming again he began to laugh and wipe his eyes afresh, and when he came he gave a kind of cry as if it were *too* much for him. It was uncommon droll, and made me laugh heartily. . . .'

Music was not neglected at Harrogate during these years. September 1839 had seen the great pianist Thalberg making 'his positively last appearance in Harrogate', and other stars to appear in the Spa Rooms were Grisi, Julius Benedict, Adelaide Kemble, Balfe, Lindsay Sloper (a pupil of Liszt's) and Louise

Nobody has served Harrogate better than Richard Ellis, seen here at the period of his third term as mayor in 1887.

Dulcken, the pianist sister of Ferdinand David for whom Mendelssohn had written his violin concerto.

The greatest musical occasion must have been that of the 6th October 1849, when the artists were Henrietta Sontag (for whom Weber and Beethoven had written major parts), Lablache (for whom Schubert had written songs and who as a fifteen year old had sung Mozart's *Requiem* at Haydn's funeral) and Thalberg, making another 'positively last appearance'.

Great as the contribution made by Dr Kennion must be accounted, the man who more than anyone deserves the title of 'Father of Victorian Harrogate' is Richard Ellis. A self-made man who having succeeded as a builder then went on to devote himself to public affairs in Harrogate, Richard Ellis was first elected as an improvement commissioner in 1855. His greatest ability lay in combining shrewd financial control with broad vision of what the town could achieve with investment and hard work. From the time of his first election until his death in 1896, he was constantly at work for the benefit of the town, and some of his earlier achievements included the adoption of the 1858 Local Government Act which enabled much needed improvement to take place: the funding and active support of the first cottage hospital; the founding of Ashville School; and the construction of an adequate system of sewerage.

Some sixteen years after the building of the Royal Pump Room, the commissioners opened another such building for the Magnesia Well in Bogs Field, which was the first step taken on the road which would eventually result in the creation of the beautiful Valley Gardens. Gothic in style, the Magnesia Well Pump Room marked a distinct break with the classical style used in most of the existing public buildings in Harrogate.

At this time Harrogate still consisted of two separate villages, although since the eighteenth century a certain amount of building had been completed along the turnpike roads via York Place to the Brunswick Inn at the crossroads, and West Park, where the most important building was Carter's lodging house. This last was built by old Nicholas Carter senior in about 1815, but was rebuilt as a fully fledged hotel in 1859. Other developments of a very restricted nature had occurred along the old footpath from Low to High Harrogate, then known as Chapel Street and since 1908 called Oxford Street. Otherwise, the huge tract of

The 'Gothick' Magnesia Well Temple of 1858 at Bogs Field, with the Royal Bath Hospital in the background.

Master builder George Dawson.

land between the two villages remained in agricultural use. In 1860 this changed.

A number of farsighted business men, including Richard Ellis and the Carter brothers, foresaw that Harrogate's future lay in developing the central area for houses, shops and hotels, and they formed the Victoria Park Company to promote the scheme. At the same time, another of the great Victorian speculator builders, George Dawson, was arriving on the scene and embarking on several projects of his own.

George Dawson was born in 1819 and passed his earliest working days as a cooper. At considerable risk to himself, he took out a mortgage on Ashfield House – traditional family home of the Thackwray family – which stood at the bottom of Montpellier Hill. He then proceeded to develop the rest of the Ashfield House estate, building in a line running from the Ginnel. Thereafter he never looked back. Dawson was fortunate in having the services of the remarkable architect J H Hirst – known as Hirst of Bristol – and their partnership produced some of Harrogate's most magnificent buildings. Numbers two to six on Parliament Street, Cambridge Crescent, Prospect Crescent, the wings of the Crown Hotel, Crescent Road, much of Swan Road and a large number of superb villas at the West End Park Estate were all built by George Dawson. Possessed of a fiery character, with a domineering sense of purpose and irrepressible will to succeed, Dawson and the improvement commissioners clashed on many an occasion, not the least of which took place after he was himself elected in 1870.

The Prospect Hotel circa 1850, with lodging houses on West Park.

The elegant Cambridge Crescent, built by George Dawson in 1867–8 to a design by J H Hirst, follows the contour of the hill in a cleverly-shaped manner.

The Magnesia Well Pump Room marked the change from classical to Gothic architecture in Harrogate.

The Congregational Church of 1861–2 flanks the entrance to Victoria Avenue.

Prospect Square a century after George Dawson's death – the legacy as strong as ever.

Queen Parade, with its lovely villas, was familiar to Alfred Lord Tennyson when he stayed at Clifton House in August 1863.

Low Harrogate as seen from the Stray about 1880.

The 1860's saw further dramatic changes. The Victoria Park Company completed its plans and opened a splendid new showpiece thoroughfare which linked High Harrogate at Queen Parade with Low Harrogate at West Park. The choice of name was obvious: Victoria Avenue.

A new central railway station was opened which linked the lines from Leeds and Knaresborough. This was negotiated with great skill by Richard Ellis, who overcame the tricky matter of the Stray crossing with the ingenious solution of putting the line in a cutting, hidden from view, and compensating for the loss of land by means of adding the site of the old Brunswick Station to the Stray. The new station opened in 1862. Unfortunately the public could only gain access on the west side, as the east side had no roads leading to it. This matter dragged on for a decade, resulting in endless bickerings and threats. Again, it was Richard Ellis who came to the rescue. He constructed a road leading from Westmorland Street right up to the east

W H Smith's bookstall at the railway station in 1882.

side of the station – East Parade – and made it over to the public, with no strings attached. He also built the fine stone houses which line the west side of the road, which was formally opened in 1875.

Considerable extensions had also been made to the old George Inn – now known as the Hotel St George – which was placed most favourably opposite the Spa Rooms and on the Ripon turnpike road. The George was owned by the Barber family, the head of which, John, was an improvement commissioner who made his reputation by being an outspoken supporter of every scheme for improving the town, but resolutely against the expenditure of public money. To his lasting credit, however, he was a great supporter for both the

East Parade was built by Richard Ellis to provide a road link with
the newly-opened Central Railway Station in 1875.

speculative development. At the same time, major improvements to the town's housing stock had taken place, thanks to the much-publicised work of the Victoria Park Company and the far more discreet but equally effective developments carried out by the Duchy of Lancaster, whose estates at the Esplanade and Beech Grove were a model of high-quality building. The main source of the town's wealth was, however, wholly in private hands, for it was the bathing and not the water drinking which produced

Alfred Lord Tennyson does not seem to have appreciated Harrogate when he came in the summer of 1863: 'We had a dreary time of it at Harrogate. The cold and damp were so great in themselves and so bad for us. . . .'

The Harrogate Hunt meeting outside the Crown Hotel around 1865. Lord Byron stayed at the Crown in 1806.

idea and financing of a market project, which Harrogate still lacked by 1870.

A greater project was, however, being planned by Richard Ellis. Progress since 1841 had resulted in the building of the Royal and several other pump rooms, the introduction of gas street lighting, sewering, road and pavement construction, a local police force and, by means of planning regulations, the control of

Richard Ellis planned James Street as a triumphal entrance to the town from the Central Station. He built the magnificent terrace seen here and gave the land on which the Victoria Monument was erected – which was also a gift from Ellis.

the highest returns, and although Harrogate had the splendid pump rooms the baths were all private.

At the end of a period of earnest debate, the foundation stone of a new and very large suite of baths was laid on the 4th February 1871 by Richard Ellis on a site next to the Old Victoria Baths. Called the 'New Victoria Baths', this venture proved one of the single most successful in financial terms ever to have been undertaken by the local authority. With a series of smaller treatment rooms placed either side of an entrance hall and two large bathing pools—one for men, one for women—the New Victoria Baths were clearly superior to the Montpellier Baths next to the Crown Hotel. In recognition of the greatly increased demand for mineral waters for bathing, large reservoirs were provided for storage purposes. At the elections of 1871, Ellis lost his seat, largely because of public disquiet at the cost of the New Victoria Baths. It was not to be the last time that the Harrogate electorate vented their spleen on an outstanding public

The New Victoria Baths of 1870 (left) replaced Williams' Old Victoria Baths of 1832 (right); the new baths were in turn replaced by Leonard Clarke in 1930 when they were converted into the Municipal Buildings.

servant in this manner, only to discover too late the value of the man they had lost. Ellis, however, bided his time, and if not quite enjoying the chaos which followed his departure he at least must have indulged in a wry smile. He was re-elected in 1872.

The private sector was not supine at this period. The Spa Rooms Company embarked on a splendid series of improvements to their estate, the chief of which was the construction of two 'Crystal Colonnades' at either side of the Spa Rooms, which were connected to a gloriously flamboyant cast-iron and glass dome straight from the *Arabian Nights*. The colonnades enabled subscribers to the Spa Rooms to take lengthy walks all round the building without disturbing events within. Palm trees and whispering fountains were also introduced, as were deck chairs. The great glass dome covered an improved pump and mineral water servery. Illuminations at night produced an altogether novel, fantastic appearance, which contemporary opinion considered vastly pleasing.

Shops in James Street built by Richard Ellis to a design by J H Hirst in the 1860's, showing a detail of the splendid colonnade.

The enlarged Spa Rooms was a monument to nineteenth century architectural taste and development. The original Greek revival building with its massive Doric columns was typical of the early Victorian – not to say Georgian – style, being a combination of strength and elegance. The extension of virtuoso cast-iron and curved glass was the product of a generation familar with Paxton's Crystal Palace. That the two dissimilar styles existed so harmoniously alongside one another was tribute to the architects who had produced them.

The embellished grounds of the Spa Rooms were the setting for 'Sylvan Concerts', which were given from 11.30 to 1.00pm, and from 8.00pm to 10.00pm. As dusk fell, the grounds (now despoiled by ugly temporary exhibition halls) were illuminated by coloured lanterns and fireworks. A skating rink was also provided and in 1875, at the zenith of the craze, Prince

Arthur visited Harrogate. He was shown round by the chairman of the company, John Barber of the George Hotel. When Barber suggested that the prince might like to try on a pair of skates, he replied: 'You are fishing for something – you may call the rink after me'. And thus it was that subsequent advertising called it 'Prince Arthur's Roller Skating Rink'.

The in-filling of central Harrogate and rise in population from 3,372 in 1841 to 6,775 in 1871 produced further calls for a market. Dr Kennion had raised the matter again in June 1861, seven years before his death, but to little effect. Ten years later, public opinion changed and the commissioners agreed to proceed. Land was acquired at favourable terms from the Carter brothers, directly opposite the new central station, and a design produced by Arthur Hiscoe. The foundation stone was laid on the 28th February 1874 by John Barber, who had been a long-time supporter of the project.

The opening ceremony was held on the 29th August 1874, and was climaxed by a dinner at the Hotel St George. Some perceptive remarks were uttered during the speeches. Barber said that 'Harrogate had made its way in spite of its inhabitants'. The astute George Dawson said he was happy to know that in the new market, 'the principle would be pursued of conducting business by weight, not by measure' (this was probably a hit at the street hawkers). Within one week, all the stalls had been taken, and a need expressed for eight more.

When the New Victoria Baths had been erected, the commissioners had received the offer of a clock from the Baroness Burdett-Coutts, but which they had deferred on the grounds that the building was not suitable for a clock tower. The market, however, was a perfect location for an impressive clock tower and the Baroness proved amenable to the idea. The famous clock-maker Potts of Leeds was commissioned, and architect Hiscoe added a beautiful tower in the Italian

Bown's 1870 extension to the Spa Rooms applied the technology of the Crystal Palace to the splendid architecture of Brighton Pavilion. All could be resurrected in the design for the new exhibition centre.

The old Harrogate Market with its splendid Italianate clock tower the day after the fire of 1914.

Renaissance style to his market, placing it at the corner of Cambridge Street where it could be seen to best advantage.

Baroness Burdett-Coutts – the richest woman in England apart possibly from Queen Victoria – had long been a visitor to Harrogate. Her first visit had been as a child in the company of her mother, a theatrical lady, who later married Coutts, the richest man in London, in 1815. When Coutts died in 1822, Harriet inherited a huge fortune. She re-married in

Parliament Street circa 1910. The turreted building marks the site of the home of Dr Deville, the formidable medical officer of health. At one time the shop to the south of Dr Deville's house was occupied by a Mr Ireland while that to the north was occupied by a Mr England, giving rise to the contemporary local saying that 'England and Ireland are divided by the devil'!

1827, when she became Duchess of St Albans. Thus two fortunes came down to her daughter Angela Burdett-Coutts, who used part of her great wealth to provide Harrogate with a market clock. A further link with the family may be found at St Albans Villa, next to the Granby. Harriet and her daughter were in the habit of staying at the Granby when in Harrogate, and so valuable was this patronage to Jonathan Benn, the proprietor, that he called his retirement villa situated next to the hotel 'St Albans'.

As the 1870's progressed, a movement grew up in the town which called for the incorporation of Harrogate as a borough. This would bring the election of a full council on a ward basis, the dignity of a mayor and, most significantly, powers for the achievement of the kind of improvements which the growing community so obviously needed. As naturally as night follows day, there were many who opposed this movement, but in the end they could do no more than

The Imperial Hotel as it looked in 1880, when it was known as the Prospect.

delay the inevitable. The big guns such as Ellis, Dawson, the Carters, and Dr Myrtle were in favour. Queen Victoria granted incorporation to Harrogate in 1884, and on Wednesday the 6th February, the charter reached Harrogate by train, brought by Mr A Malcolm Bateson, solicitor to the commissioners. Harrogate was *en fete* that day, the arrival of the train being signaled by a dramatic series of explosions from fog signals placed along the track. On the platform were waiting Richard Ellis, George Dawson, Richard Carter, Dr Myrtle and many other prominent citizens. A procession of carriages formed outside, and conveyed the charter through the streets down to the New Victoria Baths, where a dais had been erected. Harrogate had taken another important step forward.

The mood in 1884 was in contrast to that of 1841,

The genius-inventor Samson Fox, mayor from 1889 to 1892.

when the commissioners at once embarked on the building of the Royal Pump Room. Possibly in mind of the warnings expressed by opponents of incorporation, the newly-elected councillors were in no hurry to be seen as advocates for expensive projects. Nevertheless there was great confidence, and the private sector continued to develop the residential and commercial parts of the town with great aplomb. The New Duchy Estate was one such example, laid out and built by David Simpson between Cornwall Road and Ripon Road. One important step taken by the council was the purchase of the Montpellier Baths Estate in 1888, some years after George Dawson had beaten them to it. Already, the New Victoria Baths were proving too small to accommodate the huge numbers of visitors to the spa, and Ellis and his colleagues were looking to further improvements.

1887 had seen several major events in Harrogate, of which the celebrations for Queen Victoria's Golden Jubilee were by far the most important. Ellis's public spirit and great generosity had already been manifest through his gift of civic robes for all the council in 1884, as well as his construction of the Victoria Park Methodist Church and funding of the cottage hospital. Now, in 1884, he presented Harrogate with the land at the top of James Street and paid for the building of the Victoria Monument, which was unveiled with great pomp by the Marquis of Ripon. The golden jubilee was also celebrated in typical spectacular fashion by Samson Fox, who ten years previously had invented and patented a device which made him rich and internationally celebrated – the corrugated boiler flue, an ingenious method for enabling steam boilers to withstand great pressure.

Fox provided an 'ox-roasting' for the people of Harrogate, held on the Stray at High Harrogate. In glorious sunshine ('queen's weather') on Monday the 20th June 1887, the event began. For twenty-four hours the spit turned and the ox roasted. The evening was greatly enlivened. A band played, and through the gathering dusk the 'soft beams' of Samson Fox's electric lighting illuminated dancing of waltzes, polkas and quadrilles across the green carpet of the Stray. When the ox was carved at noon the following day, a crowd of huge proportions received not only the roast beef of Old England, but also portions of bread and beer. Great was the merriment as the afternoon progressed, made more colourful by the arrival of itinerant entertainers. Inspector Lumb and two constables were on hand to ensure that the queen's peace was not disturbed, which in the event was an unnecessary precaution. And, as on the previous evening, the Stray was illuminated and the band played, enabling the townspeople to 'trip the light fantastic until a late hour'.

Thus it was over a century ago on the old Harrogate Stray, when Victoria was queen.

The 1890's, a highpoint in the march of British civilization across the globe, also saw great events in Harrogate. The Stray, which since the Award of 1778 had been administered (but not owned) by holders of pasture gates, was brought under the full control of the council. This was brought about by the Act of 1893, which at a cost of £11,780 ensured that one of the town's greatest assets was firmly under public administration. The subsoil, however, remained the property of the Duke of Lancaster, a situation which has been unchanged to this day. In more recent times, suggestions for underground carparks on Stray land are all too frequent, and are made with apparent disregard for the fact that the land beneath the Stray is private property.

1896 saw the Spa Rooms Estate – so crucial for the

Crowds gathering for the 'ox-roasting' in 1887.

The Victoria Monument decorated for the diamond jubilee of 1897.

Workmen building St Luke's Church in 1897.

spa industry – being bought by the council. This was done not so much for the important mineral waters, but rather for the potential of the site as a recreation and entertainment area for the visitors. The gardens of the Spa Rooms stretched well into the Coppice Valley, where the conference centre of the 1970's was constructed. It was clearly important for this key estate to fall under full local authority control.

Ellis's last great scheme had been the promotion of the idea for an international-quality bathing and hydrotherapy centre to be built on the site of the old Montpellier Baths. When in 1895 he died, the site had already been acquired. Fortunately for Harrogate, Ellis's successor, the formidable and dynamic Charles Fortune, was at hand to further the scheme. An international competition was announced, and a brief issued which specified exactly what the council wanted. After much publicity and free and open discussion, a prize was awarded to Baggalley and Bristowe of London, whose new building, known as the Royal Baths, was opened by HRH The Duke of Cambridge on the 23rd July 1897, the year of Queen Victoria's Diamond Jubilee and a climacteric for the British Empire.

The new building was the last word in scientific hydrotherapy and luxury. Its rooms provided facilities

The Victoria Monument, gift of Richard Ellis in 1887, the year of the golden jubilee.

When opened in 1897 by HRH the Duke of Cambridge, the Royal Baths was the most advanced centre for hydrotherapy in the world.

Climax of an era: Parliament Street, the first thoroughfare in Europe to be lit with 'water gas' (one of Mayor Samson Fox's many inventions), decorated for Queen Victoria's Diamond Jubilee on the 22nd June 1897.

The central hall of the Royal Baths with its original Victorian decorations, including blue marble columns, red, green and gold stencil work and an elaborate terrazzo floor.

The interior of the Royal Baths and the oriental splendour of the
Turkish baths.

for an enormous range of treatments, with such names as schnee baths, static shock, deep peat, greville baths, D'arsonval high current, external douche, intestinal lavage and cataphoresis. Lavish quantities of fine woods, mosaic and decorative wood and plaster work were provided, as well as a great winter garden. The whole complex was a triumph of Victorian science and design. The roof even had special devices to melt the snow in winter.

At the turn of the century, Harrogate, hitherto the premier spa of the British Empire in terms of its unique variety of mineral waters and their scientific exploitation, was set to bid for international supremacy.

Having assured the town's ascendancy in the matter of spa treatment, the council had also to make provision for improved entertainment facilities, as it was recognised that for many the chief attraction of a spa was neither the water nor the treatment but the entertainments. The council had not hesitated to visit Harrogate's rivals, both in the United Kingdom and on the Continent, during the years leading up to 1900. One fruit of this was that plans were assembled for a large cure hall, or 'kursaal', which would contain a far bigger audience than could be fitted into the old Spa Rooms. Architect J R Beale provided designs which would outstrip anything in Germany or Austro-Hungary. The centrepiece was to be a 3,010 seater concert hall, around which were to be strung a series of promenades, reading rooms, smoking rooms, billiard halls, French restaurants and assembly halls, all to be constructed from the finest stone, bronze, polished mahogany and stained glass. The new building was to be set back from Ripon Road next to the Spa Rooms and connected with the 'Crystal Palace' extensions of 1870.

Alas, it was not to be. A number of irresponsible new councillors, anxious to appear as saviours of the public exchequer, cried ruin and stirred up public opinion. The result was that Beale's first scheme was thrown out, and a revised plan accepted which not only did away with the 3,010 seater hall, substituting a far smaller one with a capacity of only about 1,200, but also all the additional features such as the billiards room and French restaurant. Worse, in order to reduce the size of the connecting link with the Spa Rooms, Bown's great crystal-domed pump room was torn down to provide space for the Kursaal to be sited directly north of the Spa Rooms. This short-sighted decision, aimed at saving money, actually cost Harrogate at the very least £34 million, since there can be no doubt that had the 3,010 seater Kursaal been built, the 2,000 seater conference centre of the 1970's would have been unnecessary. One of the most difficult but necessary things for a progressive council to do is to educate the public that future prosperity depends on good investment today, and that every pound saved now may produce greater debt tomorrow.

Despite these shortcomings, the new Kursaal, opened by Sir Hubert Parry on the 4th January 1902, was a great success artistically and the cream of international celebrities appeared on its stage: Melba, Kreisler, Busoni, and Elgar, to name the greatest, all appeared at the Kursaal as glittering season followed glittering season.

The private sector was intensely active at the turn of the century. As the existing old hotels could no longer accommodate the ever-growing numbers of visitors, plans were launched for two massive establishments, the Majestic and the Grand. It was said that the former had been built as a result of a row between Sir Bundell Maple and the management of the Queen Hotel, when Sir Bundell had declared that he would build his own hotel and put the Queen out of business.

Even by Harrogate standards the new Majestic Hotel was breathtaking. Built on the site of the Carter brothers' old home, Spring Bank, it dominated the

The Royal Baths winter gardens before the construction of the lounge hall. The splendidly theatrical 'Merry Widow' staircase still survives.

Edwardian visitors to the Harlow Moor bandstand. Harlow Moor had been bought by the corporation in 1898.

Harrogate skyline, having a massive red brick and stone facade crowned with a mighty copper dome. A vast 8,000 square foot winter garden was provided, one of the biggest such in Europe (tragically torn down in the 1970's shortly before the craze for glazed conservatories arrived), and a smoking room. This last was a wonderful oriental room which had been transferred complete from the Egyptian palace of Arabi Pasha, who had hoped to rule Egypt. The Majestic was opened on the 18th July 1900, the same year as the lovely Harrogate Theatre or Opera House was completed.

Two years later, the Grand Hotel opened its doors, being sited in Cornwall Road overlooking the Valley Gardens. Harrogate was now amply provided with accommodation suited to all requirements, from the poorer invalids who stayed in the lodging houses around Cold Bath Road or Cheltenham Parade, to the great hotels such as the Crown, the George, the Granby, the Majestic, the Queen, the Old Swan, the Prospect and the White Hart.

The Old Swan had taken a different course in 1878, when it was organised as a hydro by the energetic Dr Richard Veale. Suites of hydropathic baths were constructed in the basement for guests, and a strict course of treatments introduced, consisting of plain diet, exercise, massage and regulated consumption of the mineral waters. Guests were expected to retire and rise early, join in the family prayers and to consume no alchohol. That such a regime appealed to Victorian visitors is hardly surprising!

After the setback over the Kursaal, Alderman Fortune managed to get his own way with just about every project he promoted. The great reservoir projects at Scargill and Roundhill – the latter costing the unprecedented sum of £568,000 – were forced through thanks to the unflagging energy and imperious will of their promoter. At the same time, plans for a new Royal Pump Room were being

The 18th May 1900, and news ticks through on the telegraph that Mafeking has been relieved.

examined to ease the crowding at the 1842 structure, and there was talk of a vast municipal palace in Victoria Avenue to contain the council chamber, mayor's parlour, court house, and library. These were heady days indeed.

The Municipal Palace was based on the sound proposition that land and buildings at the heart of the spa area should be used for spa purposes and not for the bureaucrats and administration. Since the opening of the New Victoria Baths in 1871, that building had provided rooms for the improvement commissioners and, after 1884, for the council. It was now suggested that the new Victoria Avenue, well away from the spa centre, should be the site for the administration. Indeed, a site had already been acquired at a very advantageous rate for the purpose, on the understanding that it would be used for nothing other than a town hall. After another competition, a design by Henry Hare was selected, in full-blown Edwardian baroque, complete with an impressive clock tower.

A start was made in 1904 when, thanks to the

The splendid interior of the Kursaal has plasterwork by Frank Matcham. Part of Ken Russell's film on Richard Strauss was filmed here.

generosity of Andrew Carnegie, the library wing of the Municipal Palace was underway. It was opened on the 24th January 1906 by Dr Kennion's son, the Bishop of Bath and Wells – an appropriate choice! However, the rest of the project was temporarily shelved when the matter of the Royal Pump Room overcrowding reached crisis point.

The dispute was between those who favoured demolishing the Royal Pump Room and replacing it with a gigantic neo-baroque structure, and those who preferred to retain the old building and enlarge it by means of a lightweight annex. Architectural taste and sentiment had nothing to do with the decision. The question was entirely on the matter of the sub-strata through which the precious sulphur water flowed. It was feared that the construction of massive foundations to take the big new building would harm the flow and possibly destroy it. In the event, supporters of the lightweight annex won the argument.

The people for whom all these improvements had

The Kursaal, renamed the 'Royal Hall' in the Great War, was given a horrible replacement canopy in the 1970's which cries out to be replaced with something more in keeping with the elegance of the sumptuous building.

Even from the rooftops the Hotel Majestic towers over Low Harrogate.

been undertaken were by and large the visitors. Although the old 'season' had run from July to September to fit in with the pattern of the London social season and the shooting in Yorkshire and Scotland, the later nineteenth century had seen its extension, and by the first decade of the twentieth century the Harrogate 'season' ran all year round. To all intents, however, the spa ritual had changed little; certain aspects had been elaborated and refined beyond recognition, but the essentials remained.

One rose early, dressed and, without having taken breakfast, walked to the Royal Pump Room where instructions from one's doctor were observed respecting the required consumption of the waters. Then, a short walk in the immediate environs of the Pump Room, around which a traffic-free zone existed for the early part of the morning. In Crescent Gardens a band played to entertain the visitors, who walked not only to take exercise but also to meet friends, to listen to the latest society gossip, admire the fashions and plan the day. In bad weather, the winter gardens or

The gorgeous spectacle of Harrogate Theatre, built in 1900 to a design by J P Briggs, today houses some of the most outstandingly creative productions in the country. It forms an essential part of the Harrogate experience and on no account should be missed.

James Street decorated by the traders for the coronation of Edward VII in 1902.

Kursaal promenades were opened. Then, at eight, the return to the hotel was made and breakfast taken. Not the least important part of medical instructions was the advice to stay in one's hotel for a while after breakfast; the strongly purgative effects of the waters made this essential.

Mid-morning was an excellent time to visit the shops, which were of London standard, virtually all private and highly exclusive. On entering, the customer would be offered a chair either at a finely polished mahogany counter or a tiny Louis Quatorze table and, after some preliminary politeness, the desired items would be brought by the assistant to the customer for inspection. Very grand customers might expect a selection of stock to be brought to the hotel

The former Grand Hotel still forms a splendid backdrop to Valley Gardens.

The palm court of the Grand Hotel with its tapestries of life in old Harrogate.

Samson Fox's oak tree opposite the ancient County Hotel, High Harrogate.

for inspection. A visit to the photographer might occur to record the visit to Harrogate. On one occasion, a well-established photographer was required to take portraits of a maharaja and his family staying at the Cairn Hydro, and on completing his task was told casually that the completed portraits must be packed in crates stuffed with rose petals.

The afternoon might bring a visit to some of the local beauty spots such as Fountains Abbey, Knaresborough or Ripon, and in the evening the day

The Royal College of Music in London, opposite the Royal Albert Hall, was paid for by the Mayor of Harrogate, Samson Fox, who took the corporation down to London in a special train for the foundation stone ceremony performed by the Prince of Wales on the 8th June 1890.

Samson Fox planting the oak to commemorate the end of the South African Wars in 1902.

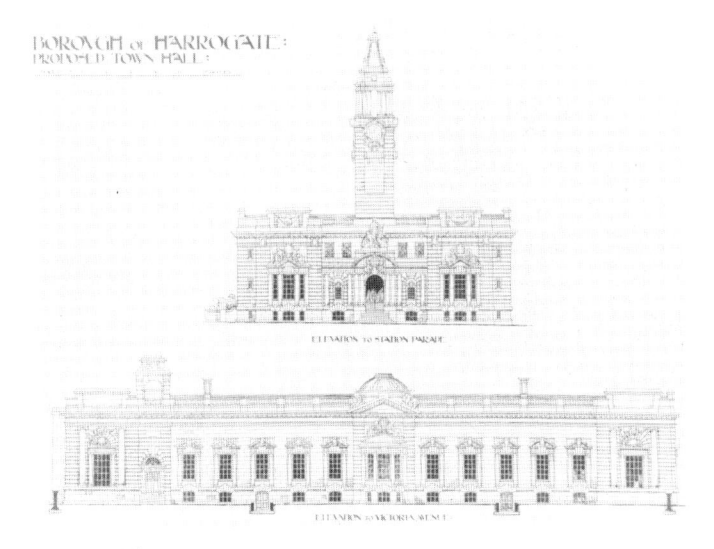

The Municipal Palace, designed by Henry Hare.

The 1st July 1903 and Alderman Charles Fortune cuts the first sod at the site of the vast Roundhill Reservoir, built at a cost of £568,268.

The dynamic Charles Fortune, worthy successor to Richard Ellis and an autocratic and imperious promoter of schemes for the advancement of Harrogate.

would be completed by a ball in one of the great hotels where superbly-dressed couples danced away the hours until early morning. The Kursaal might provide alternative entertainment, as might the Opera House, the Spa Rooms or the Empire Theatre, where a dazzling selection of variety acts performed beneath a superb hand-carved proscenium arch. For the more adventurous, the years immediately before the Great War saw flights in aeroplanes organised, some of which landed on the Stray, causing a sensation.

The special edition for the *Times and Guardian* debating the question of whether or not the Royal Pump Room should be replaced.

Harrogate transport in the days of the Raj was suitably dignified.

The early morning 'cure' in full session.

Early morning in Crescent Gardens, shortly after the daily road-washing.

Joah Baxter's splendid tobacconist's premises in James Street, immediately below Standing's Cafe.

Visitors dressed in the height of fashion enjoying an early morning stroll in Crescent Gardens during the 1911 season. Note the 'Merry Widow' hats.

June 1914 – and an aeronautical treat for the town. Mr Rowland Ding and Mr Petty land on the Stray.

Andre Beaumont's monoplane.

James Valentine in front of the Harrogate Chamber of Trade tent on the Stray.

The Harrogate Municipal Orchestra was the most important of a number of musical institutions which included Otto Schwartz and his German band and Tom Coleman and his Pierrots. That it reached very high standards of orchestral execution cannot be doubted, in view of the number of distinguished musicians who appeared as soloists with it and the enthusiastic reviews in the national press. August 1911 saw Julian Clifford conducting the first provincial performance of Elgar's Second Symphony, which received a better reception in Harrogate than London as well as a creditably perceptive review in the *Advertiser*. The following year saw Elgar conducting his *Imperial March*, the concert overture *In the South*, the *Enigma Variations*, *Chanson du Nuit*, and the delightful second *Wand of Youth* suite. He also conducted Schumann's piano concerto, played by Julian Clifford. Once again, the *Advertiser* reported an enthusiastic reception.

The season of 1911 was especially brilliant. Visitors included Queen Alexandra, Princess Victoria, the Empress Marie of Russia, Prince Henry of Prussia (the Kaiser's brother), Queen Amelia and King Manuel of Portugal, Prince Christopher of Greece and the usual smattering of cabinet ministers, archdukes and maharajas.

Never had the town been so rich and elegant, never had so much money flowed into the municipal coffers, never had the future looked so bright.

The townspeople were at this time experiencing the fruits of centuries of progress, with providence rewarding the industrious apprentice. On all fronts the spa was booming, the latest success story being the export of bottled mineral water, an activity long opposed by some on the ground that people might not visit Harrogate if they could obtain the water elsewhere. They need not have worried.

The vexed matter of the Royal Pump Room was finally settled in 1912 when plans to construct a glass

Sir Edward Elgar last visited Harrogate in 1927, when he stayed at the Hotel Majestic.

Otto Schwartz and his German band, at their pitch outside the Prospect.

and iron extension were approved. Work began almost immediately, and by the late spring of 1913 it was finished. The *Advertiser* waxed lyrical over Harrogate's happy position:

'There are many thousands of people in England who regularly turn their eyes to Harrogate. Their yearly visit to this famous Spa is the one thing that must never be omitted or postponed. Harrogate has become the vogue, not because it has practically every treatment to offer that any single Spa on the Continent can boast, but because the people who flock here seldom if ever leave disappointed.'

The extension to the Royal Pump Room was designed to accommodate these people, and special arrangements were made to celebrate its opening.

Tom Coleman and his Pierrots, a much-loved act which enlivened the streets of Harrogate.

The Harrogate lifeboat prior to launching.

These imposing mansions of the later Victorian period form an impressive boundary to South Stray.

Crown Place, with the annex to the Royal Pump Room, opened by the Lord Mayor of London with great pomp in 1913.

The morning of the 7th June 1913 was especially fine, with light from a golden sun sparkling over the domes and spires of Harrogate, illuminating the grey stone buildings, the brilliantly-coloured parks and the emerald green Stray, imparting a festive air to the people who walked the early morning streets, admiring the gay decorations which danced and shimmered in the sunlight. For the Lord Mayor of London was coming to town.

The special Harrogate Express left London at precisely 9.40am and reached the spa at precisely 1.39pm, carrying Sir David Burnett and a distinguished body of medical men. The Mayor and Mayoress of Harrogate, Councillor and Mrs J Rowntree, had for the previous hour been entertaining the other guests at a lavish luncheon in the Queen Hotel, including the Lord Mayors and Mayors of York, Leeds, Bradford, Barnsley, Beverley, Bridlington, Dewsbury, Doncaster, Halifax, Huddersfield, Hull, Keighley, Middlesbrough, Morley, Ossett, Pontefract, Pudsey, Ripon,

The temporary annex at the Royal Pump Room around 1908, showing the road closure in effect for the convenience of drinkers.

Todmorden and Wakefield, together with all the councillors and aldermen of Harrogate, the leading officials and medical men. At 1.39pm, Mayor

Station Square circa 1910.

Rowntree and the High Sheriff of Yorkshire met Sir David as his train steamed into Harrogate.

To honour the occasion, the state landau had been brought from London and was used to transport Sir David through the streets of Harrogate. After a reception at the Queen Hotel, a grand procession formed in the forecourt of that exclusive establishment. At the head stood the mounted police and the Band of the Yorkshire Hussars, accompanied by the Harrogate mace-bearer, followed by dozens of magnificent coaches bearing the dignitaries of British local government. Passing along York Place, Station Parade, James Street (where special attention had been given to decorating the monument to the deeply-

The Lord Mayor of London, Sir David Burnett, driving through Harrogate on the 7th June 1913 after the opening of the annex to the Royal Pump Room.

revered Queen Victoria), Parliament Street, and Crescent Road – and to a musical background of pomp and circumstance – the glittering procession arrived in Crescent Gardens, where a mass of townspeople and visitors had assembled.

The winter gardens of the Royal Baths had been selected as venue for the ceremony of opening the annex to the Royal Pump Room because that historic structure could not accommodate the distinguished throng gathered at 'the World's Greatest Spa'. After passing through the main entrance, the guests took their seats in the winter gardens and looked across to the beautiful curved stone staircase on which the Lord Mayor of London would deliver his speech. And when

The heart of Harrogate in 1913, looking from the dome of the Royal Baths across to the Hotel Majestic.

he spoke, it was with unabashed admiration for the municipal enterprise shown by Harrogate in developing its unique natural resources. Sir David also reminded guests that the town:

'... was not a sea-side resort, and that despite the growing number of requests for hotel rooms with a view of the sea, *no matter how high up they are,* Harrogate was clearly destined to be known as the Queen of *Inland* watering places!'

To jubilant applause and cheering, Sir David declared the annex open; outside, where the band played, the celebration could be heard and the sun still shone.

The evening of Sir David's visit saw what was

A street entertainer on the Dragon Estate in the early years of the century.

probably the most spectacular banquet – even by Edwardian standards – ever to be given in Harrogate. It was held at the Majestic and nearly 400 names had been asked as guests of the council. To an assembly brilliant with jewellery and orders seated before acres of white damask, silver and crystal, and lit by hundreds of flickering candles, the Lord Mayor of London spoke. He admitted that he:

'... was the first to admit that the citizens would be foolish to hand over their splendid natural and national assets to private enterprise. At one time the baths and wells were a hobby costing the ratepayers £2,000 a year. Today they were so profitable that during the past eight years upwards of £75,000 had been paid in redemption of loans and interest, while the rates have been relieved by the handsome sum of £11,500.'

When the banquet had come to an end, the guests left the Majestic and walked down through the grounds and into the beautifully-decorated gardens of the Kursaal and Spa Rooms, which were festooned with chinese lanterns. Melodies of the new American ragtime and waltzes by Lehar and Strauss wafted through the evening air, along with scent from the lavish floral displays, themselves enhanced by the spray from the fountains. And to climax the evening's entertainment, Harrogate's own Mr Julian Clifford, resplendent in white gloves, strode onto the Kursaal stage to conduct the Harrogate Municipal Orchestra in a programme of popular orchestral music, which included his own *Coronation March* followed by a barnstorming performance of Tchaikovsky's 1812 Overture. Incredibly, the council had also mounted an alternative entertainment in the Spa Rooms for those who did not care for music. A variety show put on by the 'Will o' the Wisps' provided lively music hall.

The new annex to the Royal Pump Room proved its value almost immediately, being full throughout the season. The following year started off well, with phenomenal bookings and an elaborate season of entertainment planned. Once again the weather was glorious, and the season had the makings of being a record.

But what was this? A clear summer's morning at the height of the 1914 season, very early, even before the band had assembled in Crescent Gardens. The town clerk's daughter, Mary Turner Taylor, on her way to her father's office to supervise an important reception later in the day. Then, cutting across the peace and silence round the Royal Pump Room, an ominous rumbling and clanking of something rapidly losing control, and which soon revealed itself to be a large trolley stacked high with luggage. Down Well Hill it rolled, gathering speed, until it eventually crashed into the sandstone wall of the Pump Room, scattering luggage everywhere, spilling packages and bursting suitcases. The silence which followed lasted a few seconds, to be broken by the sound of running and loud shouts in German. The source was the small army of German waiters who formed the main workforce at the Grand Hotel. As the early days of August ticked by and news of impending war in Europe grew ever more alarming, these waiters had decided to leave. After commandeering the luggage trolleys at the Harrogate Station, they had made an orderly early morning retreat until one of the trolleys had lost control.

The unthinkable had happened. War had broken out in Europe. After an unprecedented era of peace which had seen mighty achievements in science, the arts and social improvements, overseen by a superb sense of confidence, a catastrophe had occurred. It was all over with the old order. The curtain had come down, for Harrogate as for the whole of Europe.

Yet the war was not seen in this light by many, and as in so many communities the youth of Harrogate streamed to the recruiting office in Raglan Street in high expectations of contributing to the greatness of the hour.

Lord Derby's volunteers. Post office recruits for the Great War on parade outside Raglan Street recruiting office in 1916.

Harrogate voluntary nurses at the railway station during the Great War.

Volunteers marching round the Royal Pump Room after the outbreak of war in 1914.

The recruiting campaign at the corner of Victoria Avenue and Station Parade during the Great War.

A military parade down Parliament Street during the Great War.

Considered in the cold light of economics, the council failed to take advantage of the Great War. Although a system of providing special treatment for wounded servicemen was introduced during the later stages of the catastrophe, at no time did the council appreciate that the unprecedented number of casualties provided a golden opportunity for the spa to develop further its facilities as a rest and cure centre on a mass scale. This of course is to be wise after the event, for few could have forseen the length of the war and fewer the mortality and casualty rate. The general feeling seemed to be that the end of the war would see a return to things as they had been before 1914. Writing from a darkened London to Lady Alice Stuart Wortley in the dreadful winter of 1917, Sir Edward Elgar wrote:

'My dear Windflower, Oh! this weather & I was dreaming yesterday of woods & fields & perhaps a little drive round Harrogate – or a little play journey to Fountains or some lovely remembrance of long ago idylls – and now, deep snow.'

The Grand Duchess George of Russia presenting gifts to wounded servicemen at a reception at the Majestic during Christmas 1916.

The Harrogate tank in Library Gardens with Mayor F G Johnson standing on it.

The years following the 1918 armistice saw a hesitant approach to furthering the fortunes of the town. All of the great figures of Victorian Harrogate were dead, save for Charles Fortune, who at an advanced age lived in retirement. Physically, the fabric of the town was changed by the construction of a dramatic obelisk to serve as a memorial to the Great War. This was built on land acquired by the council from the Imperial Hotel, the foundation stone being laid by the Hon. Edward Wood MP (who later became Lord Halifax) on the 2nd June 1922. At the unveiling ceremony on the 1st September 1923, a huge crowd gathered in heavy rain and gloomy skies to watch the Earl of Harewood do the honours.

The 1920's saw considerable increases in the annual numbers of visitors, but they tended to be different to those who had come before 1914. Although the rich still visited the town, the postwar emphasis was on numbers rather than the small set of exclusive celebrities. In 1926 a record number of tickets to the Royal Pump Room were sold, and on one memorable morning 1,500 drinkers were admitted.

Harrogate still had one man with vision: Alderman Francis Barber.

In 1928 he published an impressive plan to convert the centre of Harrogate into a 'cure park' on the best continental models. The basic idea behind this scheme was that all the spa facilities should be encircled by a barrier, through which visitors could pass on payment of a fee which would then entitle them to take advantage of all treatments and entertainments available. The revenue from this 'cure tax' would be used to fund further improvements. At the heart of this scheme was the concept of Crescent Gardens being converted into a 'Forum'. The officials would be moved out of the New Victoria Baths (which would specialise in spa treatments) and a huge new assembly hall built between Swan Road and Crescent Gardens. A stone colonnade would link up all the buildings

Cambridge Street in 1919 before the building of the Scala Cinema.
The site was later occupied by the Littlewoods store.

Prospect Square in 1920 before the war memorial was built.

The 1st September 1923 and the Earl of Harewood unveils the war memorial.

The war memorial may prove to be one of the most enduring of all the constructions of the interwar years.

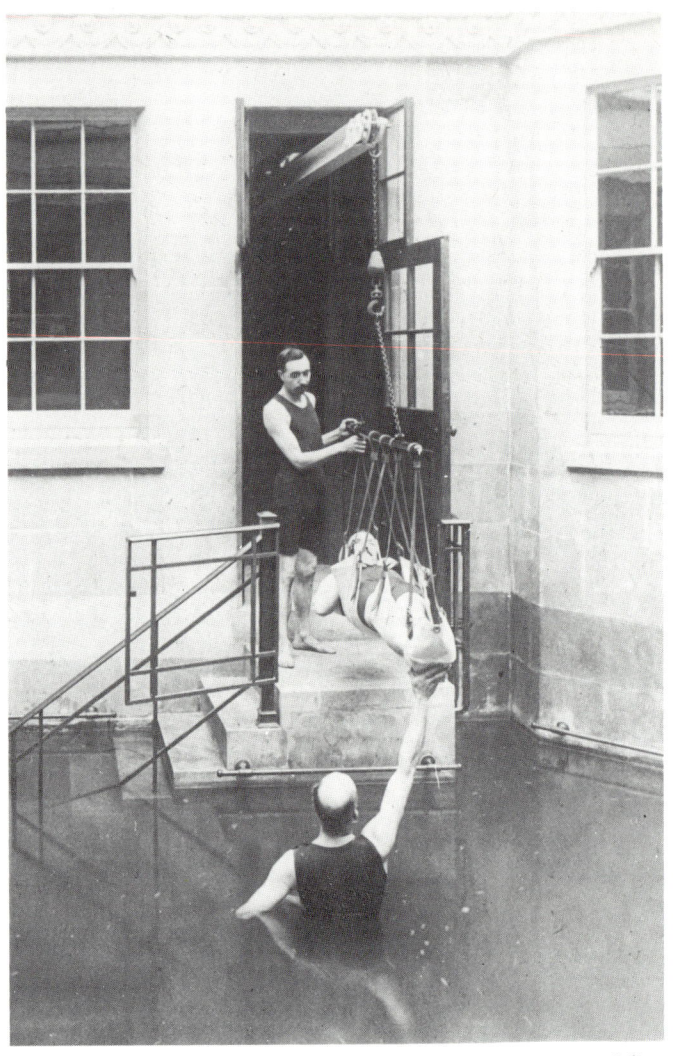

Immersion in warm peat was one of Harrogate's speciality treatments.

The Barber plan of 1928 for a Harrogate Forum.

around the 'Forum', starting at the Porte Cochere of the Royal Baths. Although the scale of the Barber scheme was too much for the council to stomach, it did stimulate much thought on the future development of the town.

A major programme of improvements had been carried out at Bogs Field in the mid-1920's. The mineral wells were provided with new brick shafts from the bedrock up to the surface of the soil. Inside, a wooden cover impregnated with wax floated on the water, enabling it to rise and fall as levels fluctuated, and thus maintain an airtight state. A heavy metal cover protected the shaft. A paddling pool and tennis courts were also constructed, in sublime indifference to the acts which required the Stray to be forever open and unenclosed.

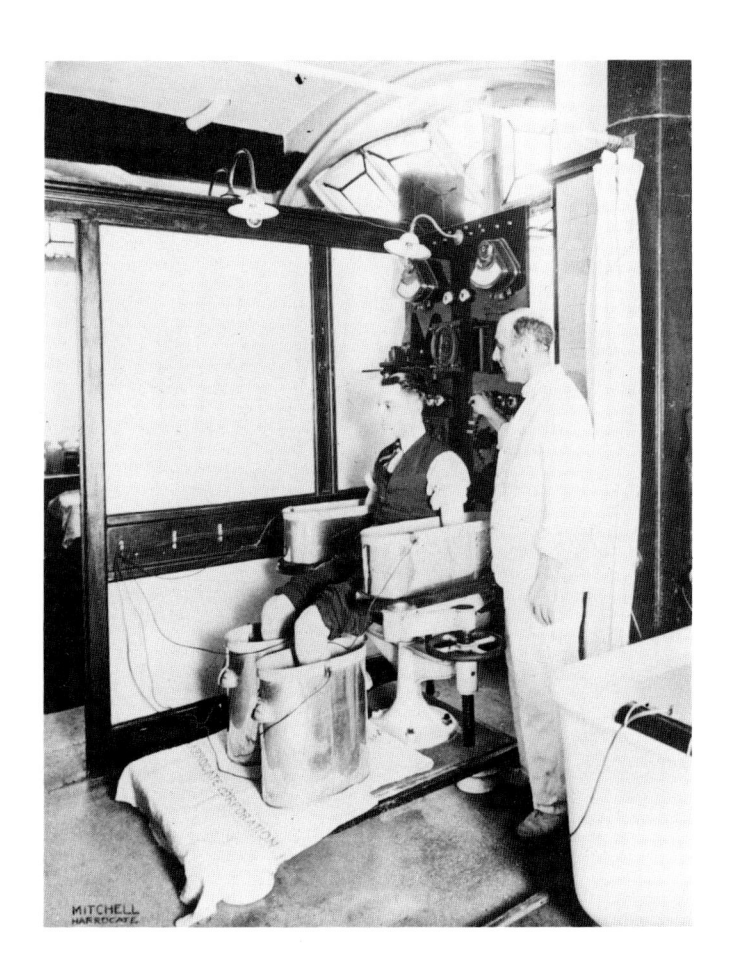

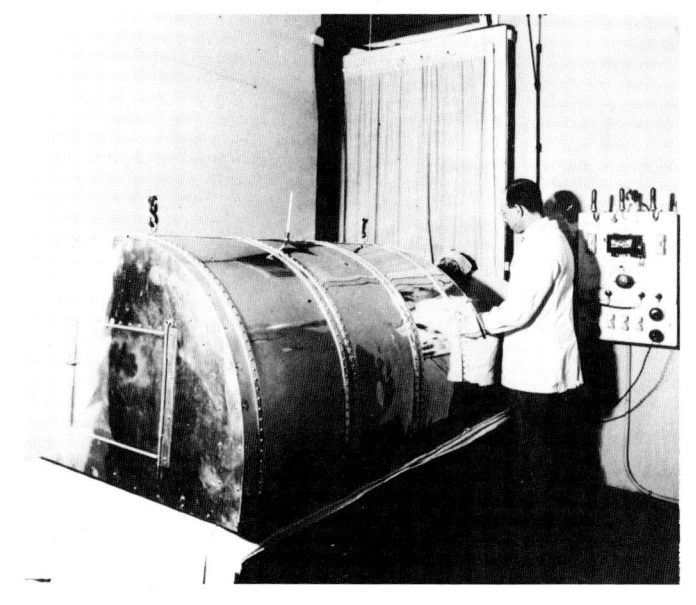

Some of the special treatments available at the Royal Baths.

visitor that Harrogate sought to attract. The fact that entertainments were stressed instead of the 'cure' was indicative of the direction the town was taking.

The Barber plan was finally rendered impossible by the conversion of the New Victoria Baths into the Municipal Buildings, opened in 1931. This was a blunder of the first magnitude, as it made permanent the incursion of the local government machine into the part of the town which should have been devoted solely to the town's only industry – the spa. The fact that the land for a town hall had been in council ownership since 1885 went for nothing – indeed the 'official' town hall site in Victoria Avenue is unbuilt to this day; henceforth all treatments would be concentrated in the Royal Baths.

Note had, however, been taken of Barber's proposals and a major scheme was submitted to link the Royal Pump Room with the Royal Bath Hospital by means of a covered walk, tea rooms, and a building

Harrogate was never reticent in promoting itself. Here is the town's pavilion at the British Empire Exhibition at Wembley in 1924.

Throughout the interwar years the North Western Railway Company and Harrogate Corporation gave careful consideration to the matter of publicity. A number of splendid posters were produced which gave the viewer no doubt whatsoever as to the type of

The Majestic in flames on the 20th June 1924; this also shows the famous conservatory which was so very popular with conference and exhibition delegates.

99

to replace the Royal Pump Room. The first stage was opened on 17th June 1933 by Lord Horder, during the hottest Whitsuntide then recorded that century. Stage two would consist of a new Royal Pump Room to be sited between the old building and the new colonnade. The third stage would see the colonnade being extended to the Royal Bath Hospital and the construction of an aviary.

The Old Swan Hotel, for centuries one of the most prestigious addresses in Harrogate, was the scene of extraordinary events in December 1926 when the missing novelist Agatha Christie was identified there. It was believed that overwork had induced a breakdown and a poster at Waterloo Station advertising Harrogate had caused the writer to journey to the spa town, where she stayed under the assumed name of Theresa Neele. Fifty years later the film *Agatha*, starring Vanessa Redgrave and Dustin Hoffman, retold the story.

The only known press photograph of Agatha Christie leaving the Old Swan Hotel after her identification in December 1926.

Was this the poster which sent Agatha Christie speeding up to Harrogate from Waterloo?

The LNER posters stressed the exclusive and fashionable nature of the Yorkshire spa throughout the 1920's and 1930's. By no stretch of the imagination could Harrogate have been described as a resort which tried to lure daytrippers or charabanc outings.

103

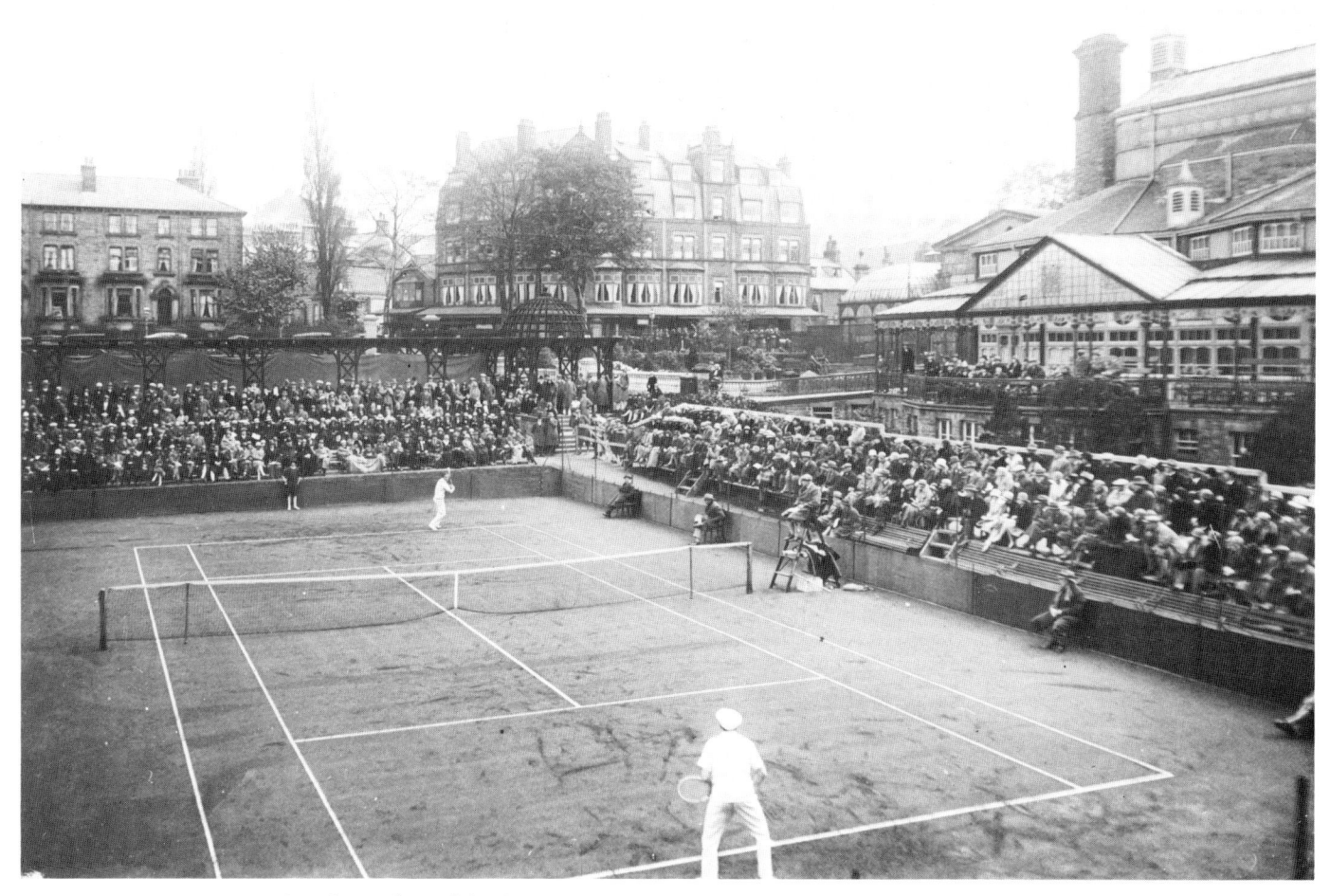

The Davis Cup being played in the gardens of the Spa Rooms on
the 8th May 1926.

A 1920's idyll in Valley Gardens.

The new paddling pool in Valley Gardens in 1928, a few yards from Bogs Field.

The Crescent Gardens bandstand in 1929, a popular meeting place for visitors.

Films were introduced to the Royal Hall for the winter season throughout the interwar years.

The new colonnade and Sun Pavilion established itself rapidly as a popular centre both for visitors and residents alike. Beneath special glass which filtered out the harmful rays of the sun, the visitor could walk along the crown of Valley Gardens and enjoy

The interior of the Sun Pavilion as it appeared in 1933.

refreshments in the beautiful Sun Pavilion with its splendid glass dome. There was more than popularity to consider, however; in terms of finance, the council could no longer afford to provide embellishment without being assured of a quick financial return.

Consequently when the great depression began to bite deeply into the British economy, stages two and three of the Valley Gardens scheme were quietly abandoned. Instead the council decided to invest in the Royal Baths Estate at the heart of the town.

An appreciation of Harrogate's financial position at this time may be obtained by examining the national returns for British spas in 1929:

Harrogate's most outstanding town clerk, J Turner Taylor, who served from 1897 to 1935.

Spa	Revenue	Expenditure	Deficiency
Bath	£17,921	£21,262	£3,341
Buxton	£10,000	£16,356	£6,356
Cheltenham	£2,516	£4,747	£2,231
Leamington	£4,426	£7,329	£2,903
Llandridod Wells	£3,654	£6,905	£3,251
Strathpeffer	'Last year the worst for 20 years – no figures released'		
Woodhall	£3,297	£6,905	£3,251

But now look at Harrogate:

Harrogate	£41,113	£39,371	£1,742 *profit*

Two distinguished visitors arrived on the 21st August 1933; King George V and Queen Mary.

Unlike all the other British spas, Harrogate had regularly invested in its facilities, both sources of direct profit such as the wells and baths, and indirect sources of profit such as parks, public seats and flower baskets. Although it would have been easy to obey the shrill calls from the ratepayers not to spend, progressive councils have always known that prosperity tomorrow requires expenditure today and that skimping leads to disaster.

The Municipal Buildings were remodelled from the New Victoria Baths in 1930.

Part of the colonnaded walk and the Sun Pavilion in Valley Gardens.

At a time when the council should have concentrated all its effort on improving the principal spa facilities and completing the three part development in Valley Gardens, a major blunder was made. Against virulent opposition from the ratepayers and in clear and flagrant breach of the 1778 Award, the council authorised the removal of large areas of West Park Stray and their replacement with flower beds and shrubberies. The response from the citizens was prompt. In 1933 a Stray Defence Association was formed. Council meetings were interrupted. On the 8th January 1934 a major debate was held in the Municipal Buildings, which included speeches from Stray Defence candidates who had been swept to power in Bilton and West Wards. Public interest was intense, and so many sought admittance, that the meeting had to move to the winter gardens, where a ladies squash meeting was under way. After a heated exchange, the ladies were removed and the meeting began in earnest. Incredibly, the original supporters of the flower bed scheme refused to acknowledge the unprecedented public hostility. The press walked out in disgust and attacked the obtuseness of the council. However, the next elections saw further Stray Defence candidates being swept to power and in November 1934 the illegal flower beds were removed and the Stray restored.

The Stray battle could not have occurred at a worse time: the council was inexperienced; the officials uncertain, due to the illness and pending retirement of the great town clerk, J Turner Taylor, who served from 1897 to 1935; the public hostile. By the time the battle was over, the council had been turned inside-out and consequently dithered over the Valley Gardens scheme.

Unfortunately the battle for the Stray has to be re-fought about once every ten years, as the Stray is regarded by many new councillors as being just big enough to permit an 'insignificant sacrifice' for whatever pet scheme they may have. Thus one councillor may have urged that 'temporary exhibition halls be erected on the Stray – they can be removed later and the grass will grow again'. Another may find that the entire traffic problems of the town may be solved by shaving a corner from Granby Corner Stray. Yet another may urge the construction of a huge boating lake near the Tewit Well. As in the past, so for ever should the public answer be 'not a blade of glass, not an inch of soil – the Stray is not negotiable'.

The last big development in Harrogate before the Second World War was the building of the western wing of the Royal Baths to provide an extended series of improved treatment facilities. At the same time as work on the site was in progress, two other developments occurred which had a profound effect on the appearance of the town – the old Harrogate Market burned down, and the Spa Rooms were demolished. A replacement market was quickly designed by the corporation's own Leonard Clarke, who had also designed the annex to the Royal Pump Room, the Sun Pavilion and colonnade in Valley Gardens as well as the new wing at the Royal Baths. Unfortunately the council's financial troubles required artificial stone to be used on all these buildings, which would produce severe structural problems before the end of the century. The loss of the Spa Rooms was the result of placing its financial status along with that of the Kursaal, with the inevitable result that the smaller, older structure always showed as a loss. When a section of the neglected cornice fell from the grand ballroom ceiling, the council used the fear of unsafety as an excuse to rid itself of the building. It was demolished in the spring of 1939, an act which must class as the single greatest deed of vandalism in the history of Harrogate. To this day the site remains a hideous eyesore. However, the columns and entablature were saved and could easily be restored to the heart of Harrogate as a grand entrance to the great

The flower beds in 1933 constructed on West Park Stray, which brought down the council. Memories, however, are short and the battle for the Stray has to be re-fought on average every ten years.

new exhibition complex currently being planned.

To emphasise the importance to the town of the extensions to the Royal Baths, the council decided to repeat the visit of the Lord Mayor of London which had been such a triumph of 1913. On this occasion, the

The Royal Pump Room continued to attract crowds of drinkers throughout the 1920's.

Removing the illegal flower beds on West Park Stray in 1934.

Sir Frank Bowater, the Lord Mayor of London, arriving at Harrogate Station on the 10th July 1939 for the ceremony to open the extensions to the Royal Baths.

Lord Mayor was Sir Frank Bowater, who came up on the 10th July 1939. Once again the state landau rolled through the streets of Harrogate and a Lord Mayor of London paid homage to the foresight of the citizens in exploiting their unrivalled natural resources for the benefit of humanity. The facilities which Sir Frank opened included a greatly extended treatment block, a 'lounge hall' decorated in elegant art deco wood panelling and a colonnaded open air fountain court. Despite the enthusiasm with which the new buildings were greeted, the dangerous situation in Europe lent a certain air of menace to the festivities. Within a few weeks the Second World War began, and the council's elaborate new extensions could not be put to the test.

The Kursaal and Spa Rooms floodlit in the 1930's.

The second market building under construction in the winter of 1938.

Exotic visitors to the Royal Baths – probably from the remoter parts of Yorkshire!

Harrogate Station in the mid 1920's.

Trenches were dug on the Stray in 1938 during the Munich crisis to prevent the landing of aircraft.

In the same year the traditional traffic barriers erected round the Royal Pump Room for the convenience of drinkers were abolished, which proved a portent.

The threat of saturation bombing and imminent Nazi invasion caused the Government to evacuate many ministerial departments to Harrogate, where the existence of an unusually high number of large hotels provided excellent accommodation. From the basement of the newly-completed Market Hall, Aldermen Bolland and Simpson ran the town under emergency powers.

On 12th September 1940 a Nazi raider reached Harrogate and dropped bombs on the Majestic, damaging the conservatory, demolishing the building at the corner of Swan Road and Ripon Road (rebuilt only in 1987), as well as causing other damage. Other visitors caused less damage, such as Churchill and Montgomery when they came in 1944.

Bombs on the Majestic on the 12th September 1940.

Bombs also demolished the villa at the corner of Swan Road and Ripon Road.

The Stray under harvest in 1940.

As the war years progressed, the appearance of Harrogate changed. The Stray was put to the plough (nobody objected) to provide food; the streets were stripped of their magnificent decorative ironwork – an action which was done purely as a government propaganda exercise, and served no other value whatsoever, as cast iron was useless for military purposes; and the general appearance allowed to deteriorate.

Plans were also made to use the Brunswick railway tunnel as a bomb shelter.

Lord Montgomery visited Harrogate in February 1944 to be greeted by the mayor, Councillor Stephenson, at the railway station.

Churchill arriving in Harrogate in 1944.

Prospect Square decorated for the coronation of the new Queen Elizabeth in 1953.

Knowing that the postwar era would bring great changes, the council commissioned Professor Davidson of Edinburgh University, to study the Harrogate spa and write a report. This was published in January 1945. The main recommendations were

125

that, as modern medical science believed it could duplicate the chemical content of the Harrogate waters and provide drugs as a replacement, there was no need to promote the natural supply. Demand for physiotherapy would certainly increase, and this service should be extended. Sporting and cultural facilities should be enhanced to attract the families of patients, and the council should make every effort to persuade the projected regional hospital authority to select Harrogate as the centre for rheumatic diseases, orthopaedics and rehabilitation.

After the war a strong reaction to the British spa set in. At Harrogate, the Royal Pump Room finally closed, to be re-opened by Lord Halifax in 1953 as a museum. The great mass of the British public, as they became more affluent, could afford to travel to sunnier climes and, perhaps most significantly, Harrogate's image as an aristocratic, exclusive spa with its solid Yorkshire buildings and old fashioned lifestyle did not attract visitors in sufficiently high numbers.

Although conferences and exhibitions had always been attracted to Harrogate – especially since the 1880's when Dr Myrtle had fought to get the British Medical Association to hold their conference in the town – it was this business which the council used as a lifeline when it became clear that the spa was going through difficulties. In 1959 a 'temporary' exhibition hall was erected on the Spa Rooms Gardens, thanks largely to the energy and foresight of W W Baxter, who went on to convince the council of the need for further exhibition halls. The cornerstone of Harrogate's economic revival had been created by 1960.

Unfortunately the council made no effort to maintain the town's traditional spa services other than the treatments in the Royal Baths, which were now part of the National Health Service. One by one the wells fell into decay, a fact which did not go unnoticed by the visitors, one of whom wrote to the *Advertiser*:

'Sir, I recently paid a passing visit to Harrogate and was amazed to see how little was done to publicise the water for which the town is renowned . . . I spent the best part of the day seeking out samples of the waters to taste, and was rewarded only with the discovery of a single sulphur well. What about the others – do they really exist? It seems that the town is missing a glorious opportunity here. . . .'

The council received one final warning about the diverging path Harrogate was taking from the thriving European spas – and from one of its own men. In 1966, Councillor Vivian Griffiths, on his own initiative and at his own expense, toured the major European spas to see how private treatments could be made to pay and to investigate the management of successful spas. This remarkably generous and public-spirited act was fully in keeping with past actions by Harrogate citizens who had gone to no small effort and expense to keep

The Spa Rooms gardens shortly before the first exhibition hall was built in 1959.

The Victoria Park Methodist Church built by Richard Ellis and now the site of the Co-op. The 1950's and 1960's saw many plans to demolish fine old buildings, but fortunately few were realised.

themselves informed of progress by rival towns. In 1966, however, it was unusually far-sighted. Baden Baden received special praise for the nature of its entertainment facilities provided for visitors, and it was noted that the casino yielded a profit to the rate payers of £26,000 a year. The *Advertiser* commented on Councillor Griffiths' tour that 'his findings are not likely to be welcome to those members of the council who would like to fold up and put away Harrogate's Spa and relegate it to the history books'.

Queen Elizabeth at the railway station on the 10th July 1957.

In the same year that Baden Baden was completing a magnificent seven story spa centre, Harrogate allowed the Tewit Well – which had been in use since 1571 – to fall into ruin. Far worse things were afoot, however.

A potentially mortal blow was delivered by the Leeds Regional Hospital Board in February 1964 when they announced that no more National Health patients would be sent to the Royal Baths after March 1968. In October 1965 the *Advertiser* published details of an interview given by the town clerk, Mr Knox, who gave the assurance that there was no question of Harrogate losing its image as the country's leading spa. Even at this late hour, one third of all British spa treatments were given at the Royal Baths. An announcement that after March 1968 the council would continue the treatments on a private basis was met with relief by many. However, within twelve months, elaborate plans had been published for a huge redevelopment scheme for the entire site. The noble building with its mighty dome would be torn down and replaced by a brutal multi-purpose 1960's style creation, which looked for all the world like a gigantic squashed liquorice allsort. Fortunately the ghastly scheme came to nothing and the Royal Baths building was saved. It was a near thing, however.

Queen Victoria turns her back on the Station Tower, an example of 1960's taste.

Today's Harrogate: superb shops, such as these in Parliament Street.

When March 1968 came round the council honoured its promise – for seven months! – before it announced that the treatment centre would close forever in March 1969. After this, the descent was swift. The news of Harrogate's fall must have been received with incredulity in Europe.

The year 1969 also saw the wrecking of the splendid pump room at the Royal Baths. The great carved mahogany servery was broken up, the magnificent mosaic floor covered over, the pumps concreted over and the area turned into a cafe – complete with plastic chairs. The taste of the time was also manifest in the new railway station. The flower-bestrewn Victorian station with its spacious forecourt and lovely iron and glass canopy was torn down to make way for a tower block in neo-brutal style.

In the meantime the historic Tewit Well had become a near ruin, and in 1973 the unique and world-famous wells at Bogs Field had their heads smashed up and submerged beneath the soil in an act of civic vandalism unparalleled since the destruction of the Spa Rooms. In a deliberate deed the council had turned a site which was – indeed still is – one of the seven natural wonders of the world into nothing more than a glorified flower bed. That this was in flagrant breach of the Act of 1770 and its successors counted for nothing. At this time the Harrogate spa reached the absolute nadir of its fortune. In less than forty years, the 'World's Greatest Spa' had become a ruin.

The transition from spa to conference and exhibition centre had, however, been undertaken so smoothly that in terms of the general economy of the town the fall of the spa was hardly noticed. In 1974 the new district of Greater Harrogate was formed which knocked at the very gates of York in the east and which embraced Boroughbridge, Knaresborough and Ripon. From the days of the fourteenth century when Harrogate had been an insignificant hamlet within the confines of the great Forest of Knaresborough, the change was dramatic.

In 1971, P A Management Consultants Ltd published their report on the future development of Harrogate as a conference and exhibition centre, the essence of which was contained in three recommendations: (1) the construction of a big conference centre; (2) the construction of additional hotel accommodation; (3) provision of better entertainment facilities for visitors.

The conference centre project was remarkably similar to those other imaginative developments from Harrogate's past, the New Victoria Baths, the Royal Baths, the Kursaal and the reservoir extensions. In each case the local authority was attempting to ensure future well-being by means of a considerable input of

No account of twentieth century Harrogate could omit Lady Frainy Dhunjibhoy Bomanji who, with her husband Sir Dhunjibhoy, made the town her principal home in 1939. Possessed of a penetrating intellect and nobility of character, her prodigious work in support of charity and the arts earned her the love and respect of many, as well as the highest honour the town could bestow: Honarary Freeman of the Borough of Harrogate.

The original market clock tower, after the 1938 fire.

Today's Harrogate: stylish and well-appointed restaurants such as Betty's, where the visitor may rub shoulders with the great and famous.

Today's Harrogate: luxury hotels, constantly striving to excel. This one, the Imperial, was opened as recently as 1988 in the building of the former Prospect Hotel which was established in 1815.

current finance and resources. In each case, expressions of public opposition were overcome by a determined effort from the promoters in the local authority. The great difference, however, between these earlier schemes and the conference centre project was that the conference centre had no Richard Ellis or Charles Fortune at the helm. Nor could the degree of public concern over the growing costs and extended

Today's Harrogate: the Club, once frequented by Sherlock Holmes (or was it Conan Doyle?), is still in existence.

The Conference Centre.

A few hardy eccentrics still consume the old sulphur water, a free outside supply of which is guaranteed by Act of Parliament.

date for completion be assuaged, because of the obsessive secrecy with which the project was shrouded. Yet when the conference centre opened in December 1981, Harrogate was in possession of a magnificent means of capturing the lucrative spin-off from the international conference business. The opening of the new International Hotel followed a few years later, thus fulfilling two recommendations of the 1971 P A Management report.

When an independent, non-council body investigated the conference centre in 1987, they found that it generated a direct income in excess of £57 million per annum through business and tourism and that it supported 3,500 full-time jobs in the district. The fact that the debt incurred by construction will take many years to pay off is not unimportant. It should, however, not be forgotten that the Kursaal took forty years to be clear of capital debt.

Tomorrow's Harrogate: Cullearn and Philips' magnificent design for the Speyhawk development of Harrogate Market, the completion date for which is scheduled for 1992.

134

The 1989 plans for the new market include a proposal to reconstruct the tower of the old 1874 market to form a 'point de vue' at the end of Cambridge Street, and an appropriate housing for the original clock presented by Baroness Angela Burdett-Coutts.

Could this be tomorrow's link with the past? The grand entrance to the new exhibition complex of the 1990's?

As Harrogate approaches the 1990's, it finds itself in a position remarkably similar to that of around 1906. Then, the newly-built Kursaal was a source of bitter contention which threatened to jeopardise necessary developments to secure the prosperity of the town (the unfinished town hall is a legacy of *that* business!); today, the quite understandable debate over the conference centre could harm the progress towards future improvements. Then, the newly opened Grand and Majestic Hotels provided a great increase in accommodation; today, the new Moat House International Hotel does the same. Then, the matter of new buildings for the principal source of income for the town (in the form of the Royal Pump Room and Baths) was being considered; today, similar considerations are being given to the redevelopment of the exhibition halls, which are beyond question the single most important element in the local economy.

If Harrogate has been fortunate in such assets as the wells, the Stray and its stock of public buildings, it has been equally blessed by the contribution of a number of outstanding citizens. These individuals may not have been liked by the majority for their single-minded and often ruthless pursuit of their vision of Harrogate, but they were invariably respected. That the town has never been without such men may in the last analysis prove to have been the greatest asset of all.

Postscript in the Underworld

And having established this bond, we shall share a secret. Let us draw the brackets round, to ensure the secret is kept. (In November 1988 a journey of exploration was taken into a dark and crumbling cellar, where, with the aid of torches and a faded map, a number of locations were identified on a stone floor. After clearing away piles of broken furniture, planks, and the detritus of ages, a dark metal lid revealed itself. Force and coaxing, and the lid opened. The torch beams stabbing down into inky blackness, revealing the shaft of a well, lined with brick, in immaculate condition. With a companion's help, further sites were found, further shafts uncovered. And in each, the beams revealed not just a shaft, but fifteen to twenty feet of glittering water, some tinged faintly with blue or green. For the waters of Harrogate still flow and dance in their neglect.)
I know, for I have seen them.

Malcolm G Neesam

BIBLIOGRAPHY

G Capel *Harrogate as it Was* Hendon 1972

W Grainge *History and Topography of Harrogate and the Forest of Knaresborough* Russell Smith 1871 Reprinted 1989

W Haythornthwaite *Harrogate Story* Dalesman 1954

B Jennings (editor) *History of Harrogate and Knaresborough* Harrogate WEA Local History Group.

M G Neesam *Harrogate in Old Picture Post Cards* European Library 1983

M G Neesam (editor) *Thorpe's Illustrated Guide to Harrogate* Chantry Press 1986

Patmore, J A *Atlas of Harrogate* Harrogate Corporation 1963

H H Walker *Harrogate's Past* Ackrill Press 1959

H H Walker *The History of the Harrogate Stray* H H Walker 1978

H H Walker completed by M G Neesam *History of Harrogate under the Improvement Commissioners, 1841–1884* Manor Place Press 1986